Robert W. Uphaus

BEYOND
TRAGEDY

Structure & Experience
in Shakespeare's
Romances

THE UNIVERSITY PRESS OF KENTUCKY

MSK 82-302

Library of Congress Cataloging in Publication Data
Uphaus, Robert W.
   Beyond tragedy
   Includes bibliographical references and index.
   1. Shakespeare, William, 1564-1616—Tragicomedies.
I. Title.
PR2981.5.U6   822.3'3   80-5184
ISBN 0-8131-1441-1   AACR2

Scholarly publisher for the Commonwealth,
serving Berea College, Centre College of Kentucky,
Eastern Kentucky University, The Filson Club,
Georgetown College, Kentucky Historical Society,
Kentucky State University, Morehead State University,
Murray State University, Northern Kentucky University,
Transylvania University, University of Kentucky,
University of Louisville, and Western Kentucky University.

Editorial and Sales Offices: Lexington, Kentucky 40506

FOR SUE

I cannot be Mine own,
nor any thing to any,
if I be not thine.

CONTENTS

ACKNOWLEDGMENTS

I wish to thank the editors of *The Centennial Review* and the *Iowa State Journal of Research* for allowing me to reprint portions of my book, and I am grateful for the financial help I have received from both the College of Arts and Letters and the All University Research Fund at Michigan State University. My wife, Sue, in so many ways makes this book possible.

But the question which too few ask is, what kind of emotional response were the Romances designed to arouse? Has not the "delight" of romance been rather neglected?

—Philip Edwards, "Shakespeare's Romances: 1900-1957," *Shakespeare Survey* 11 (1958): 17.

ONE

Beyond Tragedy

The argument of this study is easy enough to describe, but perhaps more difficult to execute. Although one critic has cautioned that "if the literary genre of romance can be defined—or described—it is not by formal characteristics,"[1] I shall argue that in at least five fundamental ways Shakespeare's romances represent and enact a realm of human experience which can be said to be "beyond tragedy."

Customarily tragedy has been regarded as the be-all and end-all of human and dramatic experience. Whether one argues that tragedy deals with "'boundary situations,' man at the limits of his sovereignty," or that tragedy presents a conflict between "necessity, and the reaction to necessity of self-conscious effort," or that tragedy is always marked by a turn toward an absolute close,[2] there still remains a strong, if unsuspected, conviction that tragedy is the most important form of drama because it is the drama of the greatest human magnitude. That magnitude is directly related to the fact that tragedy deals with death, an event of the greatest human importance, and in dealing with death tragedy takes up, paradoxically, the most basic issue of life: namely, the meaning and value of life itself. Indeed, the presence of death in tragedy defines the magnitude, meaning, and value of life. When Wallace Stevens writes that "death is the mother of beauty," or Emily Dickinson says that "after great pain a formal feeling comes," they are both suggesting the essence of tragedy as we know it in Western culture. That is, the aesthetic enactment of death formalizes and defines life's beauty. Death is our "mother" in the sense that the moment we are born is the moment of greatest human suffering in potential, and the tragic pattern of life is the realization and exhaustion of that potential.

Maud Bodkin describes this pattern quite precisely when she argues that "the archetypal pattern corresponding to tragedy may be said to be a certain organization of the tendencies of self-assertion and submission. The self which is asserted is magnified by that same collective force to which finally submission is made; and from the tension of the two impulses and their reaction upon each other, under the conditions of poetic exaltation, the distinctive tragic attitude and emotion appears to arise."[3]

To put it another way, in tragedy we live dying. What gives tragedy its peculiar power is that it represents not so much a chosen death, as a death which formally elicits and circumscribes the tremendous potential of human accomplishment. The magnitude of tragedy is defined by the greatest individual achievements, and the greatest achievement of life, in tragedy, is to die a death which expresses the fullest experience and awareness of the terrible loss it is to lose a life.

Above all, tragedy as we know it depends on the characters' and audience's commitment to life as a supreme value. It would be impossible, at least in Western culture, to write a successful tragedy if either the audience or the characters did not believe in, nor assert, the continuation of human life. For if they did not believe in life and its perpetuation of significant value, then death would be inconsequential, both humanly and dramatically speaking. Death is thus the turn toward an absolute close, because death in tragedy defines life's significance at the same time that it represents the loss of life's significance. The tragic protagonist, such as King Lear, dies into life ("we came crying hither"), even as he lives into death. The tragic conclusion of *King Lear* demonstrates that the meaning of the play and of human life is ultimately defined by the loss or exhaustion of the very life which asserts that meaning.

But what happens to a tragic sense of life when the conventional basis of tragedy is at once reversed and expanded? That is, in tragedy life or the will to live is eventually the cause of death. But what do we say about a kind of drama which is largely based on the idea that death is the cause of which life is the ultimate effect? Suddenly, what was an absolute close becomes a fascinating entrance into a different realm of human experience, a prelude, in fact, to the continuation and regeneration of life. For such a sense of continuation to occur, the value and magnitude of an individual life, on which tragedy is based, must be supplanted by, or rather incorporated in, a new set of values and experiences which assert the predominance and continuation of the life cycle generally, even as they limit the value of specific individual lives. This sense of continuation, which includes but does not repudiate the conventions of tragedy, is the basis of Shakespeare's romances.

I am not, of course, the first person to suggest that Shakespeare's romances go "beyond tragedy," but I do not think the implications—structural and experiential—of this perception have been systematically worked out. Nevertheless, my approach is greatly indebted to the work of such people as E. M. W. Tillyard, who argues that Shakespeare's last plays "develop the final phase of the tragic pattern," G. Wilson Knight, who associates the final plays with a "beyond tragedy recognition," and Howard Felperin, who more recently has argued that "Shakespeare's final romances subsume tragedy in the process of transcending it." Moreover, Norman Sanders is quite correct in describing the basis of Northrop Frye's approach to the romances as one which assumes that "the romances can take us, as myth took our ancestors, beyond tragedy and into the participation in a higher order of reality that all men desire."[4] But by focusing specifically on the various ways in which Shakespeare's romances go beyond tragedy, I hope to prevent my study from succumbing to Philip Edwards's apt condemnation of the Myth, Symbol, and Allegory approaches to Shakespeare's romances: namely, that the members of this school "are united in the belief that the Romances are written in a form of other-speaking."[5]

Of the many definitions of romance, there are three which strike me as being most suggestive in their understanding of how romance incorporates and goes beyond tragedy. John Danby has written that the romance world "has four spheres that are interlocked. There is first the sphere of virtue and attained perfection; then the sphere of human imperfection, political and passionate, surrounding and likely at any minute to threaten the first; around these again, the sphere of non-human accident, chance, or misfortune, the sphere of the sea and storms; and finally, enclosing all, the sphere of the transcendent, guaranteeing after the 'storm and other hard slights' that the ending will be a happy one—granted patience." Where Danby emphasizes the inclusiveness of romance—that is, its capacity to absorb diverse experiences as well as diverse genres—Frank Kermode focuses on the fragility and selectivity of romance. He defines romance as "a mode of exhibiting the action of magical and moral laws in a version of human life so selective as to obscure, for the special purpose of concentrating attention on these laws, the fact that in reality their force is intermittent and only fitfully glimpsed." And J. R. R. Tolkien, who acutely distinguishes Joy "as the mark of the true fairy story (or romance)," explains how this experience of Joy is actually heightened by the presence of tragedy: "In its fairy-tale—or other world—setting, [romance] is a sudden and miraculous grace: never to be counted on to recur. It does not deny the existence of *dyscatastrophe,* of sorrow and failure: the possibility of these is necessary to the joy of deliverance; it denies (in the face of much evidence, if you will) universal final defeat and in so far is *evangelium,* giving a fleeting glimpse of Joy, Joy beyond the walls of the world, poignant as grief."[6]

   In surveying the five distinct but interrelated ways in which Shakespeare's romances represent a realm beyond tragedy, a realm "beyond the walls of the world" as Tolkien says, let us consider first the least persuasive way: the chronological position of the romances. Although the exact dates of Shakespeare's plays are conjectural, there is general agreement that such plays as *Macbeth, King Lear,* and *Antony and Cleopatra* immediately precede Shakespeare's romances. What makes these plays, as well as their chronological position, extremely interesting is that compared to, say, *Hamlet* and *Othello,* these plays have frequently been thought of as problematic tragedies. They are peculiar plays, which tend not to abide by the conventions Shakespare employs in the earlier tragedies. Indeed, it appears that such plays as *King Lear* and *Antony and Cleopatra* straddle two worlds: the world of tragedy as we know it from Shakespeare's prior tragedies, and a second world, beyond tragedy, which is implied in *Macbeth*, intimated in Act IV of *King Lear*, and enacted throughout *Antony and Cleopatra*.

As will be apparent in the next chapter, however, I am not suggesting that *Macbeth*, *King Lear*, and *Antony and Cleopatra* are something other than tragedy. Rather they are tragedies that either intimate or dramatize versions of "worlds elsewhere," to borrow from *Coriolanus*, and, further, these "worlds elsewhere" subsequently become the experiential realm beyond tragedy which is fully enacted in the romances. The chronological position of these late tragedies suggests the very straddling quality which I believe to be characteristic of some of the dramatic effects in *King Lear* and *Antony and Cleopatra*.

The second way in which Shakespeare's romances may be seen as dramatizing a realm beyond tragedy is in the assumptions common to their genre. Tragedy, as I argued earlier, is determined by the value it places on the potential and exhaustion of human accomplishment, which is its source of magnitude, and by its turn toward an absolute close. All choices enacted by Shakespeare's tragic protagonists are irreversible; we see in tragedy Robert Heilman has remarked, "the inevitability of the avoidable." Shakespeare's tragic protagonists are trapped within time, and thus, to use Northrop Frye's phrase, they become fools of time.[7] The absolute close of tragedy is the dramatic concomitant of the character's experience of time, and there is no exit available for Shakespeare's tragic protagonists from time's one-directional, and essentially destructive, movement.

But Shakespeare's romances do provide an exit from the seemingly irreversible movement of the tragic experience of time by continually presenting the characters, as well as the audience, with versions of a second chance or fresh start. The romances achieve this exit by adopting two different premises that are wholly antithetical to—and yet capable of assimilating—tragedy. First, the value accorded to individual human life is replaced by an emphasis on the cycle of life and death as a continuation of the larger processes of life itself. Human nature, so to say, is supplanted by "great, creating Nature," and death is seen to be a prelude to the larger regenerative processes of the total life cycle of nature. Although this strategy bears some resemblance to Shakespeare's use of pastoral in his earlier comedies, I shall try to show, especially in my discussion of *The Winter's Tale,* that pastoral is not simply used as a "green world," where characters clarify and simplify the threatening complexities of an urban or court world; rather, in the romances pastoral serves as a crucial transition or stage between a prior tragedy and the subsequent experience of romance. If the use of pastoral in Shakespeare's comedies contributes to the principle "through release to clarification,"[8] one might say the romances use pastoral as a bridge "from tragedy to providential revelation."

Dramatically, this movement away from human nature to great creating Nature may also be seen in the romances' drift away from psychological experience, which is distinctly realistic and individual, to archetypal patterns of human behavior which emphasize the collective and symbolic patterns of the life cycle. Thus the romances frequently place great importance on such things as the sea, flowers, music, seasonal cycles, magic, and transrational experiences generally, where human activities are subsidiary to, though linked with, the processes of life itself. In the romances, human consciousness is repeatedly transformed into a kind of symbolic or emblematic awareness, and many of the central characters—especially the women—are associated with the abstract virtues of patience, charity, chastity, faith, and truth. This is not to deny the identity of the characters as people, however; many of the romances, as C. L. Barber has noted, involve "the transition of persons into virtually sacred figures who yet remain persons."[9]

Similarly, to achieve this movement away from the psychological and individual to the archetypal and communal, Shakespeare departs from the tragic sense of time. Instead of treating time as leading always and only toward death, or as irreversible, the romances continually, and often abruptly, depend on versions of reversible time, where the ideas of cause and effect, beginning and end, are displaced by a sense of simultaneity, harmony, and hierophany. Some of these disruptions of conventional uses of time no doubt derive from the tradition of Greek romance, as this tradition has been described by

Samuel Lee Wolff, Moses Hadas, Ben Edwin Perry, and Carol Gesner.[10] No less important, though, Shakespeare's use of reversible
time is quite unlike the dominant image of time in his sonnets. In
the sonnets Shakespeare continually emphasizes "wasteful Time"
(Sonnet 15), "this bloody tyrant Time" (Sonnet 16), "Devouring
Time" (Sonnet 19), and "sluttish time" (Sonnet 55) because the basic understanding of time in the sonnets is that "In sequent toil all
forwards do contend" (Sonnet 60).[11] That is, time is essentially one-
directional, leading from birth to death.

Now it is certainly true that Shakespeare also writes sonnets
about the potential immortality of his "pow'rful rhyme" (Sonnet
55), and he also suggests that "nothing 'gainst Time's scythe can
make defense / Save breed" (Sonnet 12). But the principal difference
between the dominant use of time in the sonnets, as distinguished
from the romances, is that in the former we are insistently reminded
of "Time's thievish progress to eternity" (Sonnet 77), while in the
romances Shakespeare works variations of the idea expressed in *The
Rape of Lucrece* that time is also a "ceaseless lackey to Eternity." Indeed, as Erwin Panofsky reminds us, "the figure of Father Time
. . . may act, generally speaking, either as a Destroyer, or as a Revealer, or as a universal and inexorable power which through a cycle of procreation and destruction causes what may be called a cos-
mic continuity."[12] It is precisely this principle of continuity, often
expressed through mother-daughter relationships, that enables
Shakespeare to use reversible time in the romances as a way of going
beyond, without repudiating, the experience of tragedy.[13]

Furthermore, unlike tragedy, where the characters' time sense is
essentially temporal because "In sequent toil all forwards do contend," the romances draw on sacred experiences of time. Remark-
ing on *The Winter's Tale*, Brian Cosgrove has noted: "Besides the
idea of values *in time*, it is also possible to find in the play intimations of values which *outstrip time*. In other words, there are sugges-
tions of a realm of transcendent value which time cannot touch."
Characters thus do not so much control as respond to experiences
larger than their own lives and defiant of strictly rational comprehension. For example, Kenneth Semon has observed about *Pericles*:

"Only when one accepts the events without trying to explain or control them does one come to some kind of understanding; and that understanding is always beyond any rational explanations."[14] Such an awareness in the romances is invariably prompted by the intrusion of oracles, visions, dreams, or experiences of apparent madness, where characters are lifted out of themselves and their conventional sense of time to an experience of the transcendent and sacred wholeness of life.

The structural equivalent of these two premises is the third characteristic of Shakespeare's romances. In these plays the plot structure moves beyond tragedy and projects a sense of destiny in the guise neither of Fate nor of Fortune, but of Providence. The plot structure of the romances literally enacts a movement beyond tragedy by first positing the existence either of tragedy or of an event with tragic potential, and then moving beyond it to unfold a process of destiny which culminates with a providential experience, of one kind or another, that absorbs the existence of, or potential for, tragedy. This process can be clearly seen if we briefly recall the plots of the various romances.

Pericles begins with the taboo which, Claude Lévi-Strauss has suggested, cuts across all human cultures as the ultimate violation of kinship patterns—incest. It is this taboo, either in fact or in potential, which is the source of such tragedies as *Oedipus Rex, Hamlet,* and, perhaps arguably, *King Lear* and *Coriolanus.* All the disruptions of *Pericles* seem to flow, directly or indirectly, from this primal threat to family and social structure. The presence of incest serves as an example of a pattern that prevails in the romances: C. L. Barber points out that the "late romances deal with freeing family ties from the threat of sexual degradation."[15] Thus *Pericles* begins with an event of potentially tragic significance, but proceeds beyond the threat of tragedy to a concluding hierophany at the temple of Diana. *Cymbeline* and *The Winter's Tale* also begin with kinship disruptions of enormous tragic potential—the separation of husbands and wives, fathers and daughters, fathers and sons—but these displacements again do not lead to an absolute close; rather they become the backdrop and prelude to an experience of providential order. Here *The Winter's Tale* is a spectacular example of romance's ability to elicit a human and dramatic experience beyond tragedy; for Acts IV and V, through the use of pastoral comedy as well as the reversal of tragic time, modulate the genuine tragedy of Act I–III.ii into the realm of romance, culminating with the great statue scene in V.iii which incorporates—without repudiating—the tragic loss of the previous generation. In *The Tempest* Shakespeare works yet another plot version of romance as beyond tragedy by constructing a play around the tragic events of twelve years past, so that the whole of *The Tempest* is at once a reenactment and a recycling of a past tragedy that leads to an experience of romance, as transformed tragedy, in the present. For Prospero and the older generation, the entire play enacts a second chance whereby the characters' tragic past is incorporated into a redeemed present beyond tragedy. And *Henry VIII*, which I shall argue is basically a romance, begins with the potentially tragic deaths of Buckingham, Wolsey, and Katherine, only to treat these events as preludes to the birth of Elizabeth and the rise of Protestantism, which events absorb tragedy and occasion Cranmer's providential reading of how history verifies the dramatic experience of romance.

These plot structures, however, frequently place a great deal of strain on the audience's, as well as the critics', conventional expectations. For one thing, the plot structures of the romances do not conform with our ordinary understanding of reality, either experientially or critically. These two matters—the requirement of the ability and willingness to experience romance, and the strain on our critical vocabulary in light of this the experience—make up the fourth and fifth characteristics of the romances' unique representation of a world beyond tragedy. Unfortunately, it is difficult to sort out, even analytically, the experience of romance from the critical ability to write about romance, simply because these matters so heavily influence one another. The central problem is that our ability to experience and to write about romance is principally determined by our assumptions, conscious or unconscious, about what constitutes reality, both in fact and in drama.

Shakespeare's diverse uses of tragedy, comedy, and history generally abide by our ordinary sense of reality. I say "generally," because *Hamlet* and *A Midsummer Night's Dream* are two relatively early plays which are problematical. Even so, as structural definitions—subject, of course, to considerable debate—I would argue that these three forms of drama respectively project a sense of destiny in the guise either of fate, fortune, or chronicle. Tragedy, comedy, and history are based on three well-known and easily verifiable facets of human activity: the death of individuals, the survival of individuals, and the death and succession of royal and historical personages. Shakespeare's history plays are perhaps the most conspicuously verifiable in the sense that they chronicle, even as they reshape, the recorded events of past history. But as Christopher Fry has shrewdly observed, tragedy and comedy also draw on known patterns of human behavior: "The difference between tragedy and comedy is the difference between experience and intuition. In the experience we strive against every condition of our animal life: against death, against the frustration of ambition, against the instability of human love. In the intuition we trust the arduous eccentricities we're born to, and see the oddness of a creature who has never got acclimatized to being created." [16] In other words, the basic structure of these dramatic forms retains at least a minimum of probability, in that it is founded on and elicits a sense of what could conceivably happen in ordinary life. Hence, the genres of tragedy, comedy, and history are not basically defiant of the audience's sense of reality.

But the romances are openly defiant of probability, both dramatic and historical. They defy our conventional assumptions about reality and rationality by dramatizing a realm of experience beyond what customarily passes for reality and beyond, therefore, the grasp of a critical vocabulary whose basic premise is the self-sufficiency of reason. It is awareness of this that has led Brian Cosgrove to remark about the effect of *The Winter's Tale,* "It is, finally, the spectator-critic who is excluded from the center of the play, the imaginative participant who enters into it." [17] This does not mean that my approach to the romances is fated to be fundamentally intuitive—an approach, as it were, that would emphasize vibrations rather than perceptions. In dramatizing a world beyond tragedy, the romances implicitly challenge and enlarge our ordinary expectations about literature and reality, and this challenge is—or should be—one of their chief delights. One starting point for acknowledging the implications of this challenge is to examine the diverse ways through which the romances project a realm of human and dramatic experience beyond tragedy, even as they draw from Shakespeare's prior tragedies to enact such a unique experience.

TWO

Tragedy and
the Intimations
of Romance

Many critics have noted significant relationships between Shakespeare's last tragedies and the romances.[1] Just as the romances chronologically follow a number of tragedies, so experientially and dramatically they draw from tragedy as the necessary prelude to the experience of romance. In this chapter I shall consider the spectrum of tragic structure in some of Shakespeare's later tragedies and argue that while *Macbeth* is an orthodox tragedy, *King Lear* and *Antony and Cleopatra,* defined against *Macbeth,* introduce elements which intimate the idea of Shakespearean romance and, just as important, define that idea against the structure and experience of tragedy. By looking at three of the late tragedies I shall try to determine the basic premises of the plays' tragic structure and to show how this structure is expanded by the introduction of elements which later contribute to the unique form of Shakespeare's romances. I shall suggest that *King Lear* and *Antony and Cleopatra* intimate or dramatize versions of "worlds elsewhere,"[2] and further, that these "worlds elsewhere" subsequently become the experiential realm beyond tragedy which is fully enacted in the romances.

As I indicated in chapter 1, Shakespeare's tragedies are based on at least five elements. First, the overall action of the play displays the protagonist in a "boundary situation," or as Richard Sewall says, "man at the limits of his sovereignty." Second, this tragic action gives rise to a tension between what Maud Bodkin calls the vying tendencies of "self-assertion and submission," in which the tragic protagonist finally submits to necessity. Third, the magnitude (intellectual, social, psychological, political) of the tragic protagonist serves to define and heighten the value of human life, even as the protagonist, paradoxically, attempts to destroy and consume that value. Fourth, the tragic protagonist experiences time as irreversible—that is, he is denied a second chance—though there are non-Shakespearean tragedies, such as *Oedipus at Colonus* and *Samson Agonistes,* where this is not the case. Fifth, the protagonist's action in time exists within a dramatic structure that inevitably moves toward an absolute close—usually death.

For example, from the very beginning *Macbeth* presents the audience, as well as Macbeth, with a striking series of equivocations which elicit a need for definition and resolution. These equivocations, though they antedate Macbeth's presence on stage, require his presence for clarification. Moreover, it is against this equivocal backdrop that Macbeth, as the ultimate clarifier, defines the experience of tragedy as he attempts to assert control over what looms as necessity. When Banquo and Macbeth in I.iii hear the witches' prophecy that Macbeth will become Thane of Cawdor, as well as King, Banquo asks the witches to "look into the seeds of time, / And say which grain will grow and which will not" (I.iii.58-59). Banquo's question stimulates the subsequent direction of the play and forces the witches to distinguish between what is, ultimately, tragic and what is nontragic. The "seeds of time," it turns out, are themselves equivocal: "Lesser than Macbeth, and greater / Not so happy, yet much happier. / Thou shalt get kings, though thou be none" (65-67).

The first thing to notice here is that Banquo's question and the witches' response draw on a distinction between a compressed and an expanded view of time, between the short run and the long run. The short-run view, which appears favorable, is in fact tragic because it will lead to an absolute close; the long-run view, which looks unfavorable, is ultimately nontragic because it forecasts future recovery. Both these views further draw on an equivocal sense of growth: Macbeth's grains will grow to death and cease—the absolute close of tragedy. Banquo's grains will grow and prosper—his sons, according to legend, will become the Stuart line, though he will die. In this instance, the value of individual life is poised against the cycle of life itself. Macbeth wishes to possess, by an act of self-assertion, that which is of value to individual life—in his case, immediate political power; whereas Banquo's lack of tragic assertion ultimately defines a more stable future value—the perpetuation of his family line. In the one case possession defines loss and the cessation of growth; in the other case, lack of possession defines gain and future growth.

This pendulum swing from the tragic to the nontragic is precisely expressed in the witches' answer to Banquo which plays on the diverse understandings of tragic, irreversible time, and nontragic, reversible time. Banquo's individual fate is, in the short run, lesser and not so happy as Macbeth's; while in the long run it is greater and much happier because, unlike Macbeth's absolute close, Banquo's individual death is a prelude to the line of kings he has begotten. In this respect, Lady Macbeth's later assertion, "'Tis safer to be that which we destroy / Than by destruction dwell in doubtful joy" (III.ii.6-7) alludes to the difference between the expansive view of nontragic time, and the shorter, compressed view of tragic time. Thus the respective fates of Macbeth and Banquo are not duplicates, though both men die, but opposites. But the play itself, with Macbeth as its center, deals only with the compressed time of tragedy, where every action Macbeth initiates in the present is done in anticipation of, and defined against, future necessity. Every act of possession defines what Macbeth values most about life, but draws him irreversibly toward an absolute close.

This irreversible and equivocal logic of tragedy may be seen if we look at three points in the play which, respectively, show Macbeth's seeming possession of "all," his need to destroy "all," and the ultimate effect of his actions which, in diverse ways, amounts to "nothing." At the beginning of Act III Banquo declares:

> Thou hast it now: King, Cawdor, Glamis, all,
> As the weird women promis'd, and I fear

Thou play'dst most foully for't; yet it was said
It should not stand in thy posterity,
But that myself should be the root and father
Of many kings. If there come truth from them—
As upon them, Macbeth, their speeches shine—
Why, by the verities on thee made good,
May they not be my oracles as well
And set me up in hope. (III.i.1-10)

In Act IV Macduff, hearing of the death of his wife and children, grieves over their loss:

He has no children. All my pretty ones?
Did you say all? O hell-kite! All?
What, all my pretty chickens, and their dam,
At one fell swoop? (IV.iii.216-19)

And in Act V Macbeth, told of his wife's death, contemplates the unfolding pattern of his tragic destiny:

She should have died hereafter;
There would have been time for such a word.
To-morrow, and to-morrow, and to-morrow
Creeps in this petty pace from day to day,
To the last syllable of recorded time;
And all our yesterdays have lighted fools
The way to dusty death. Out, out, brief candle!
Life's but a walking shadow, a poor player,
That struts and frets his hour upon the stage,
And then is heard no more. It is a tale
Told by an idiot, full of sound and fury,
Signifying nothing. (V.v.17-28)

In the first speech, Banquo's assertion concerning Macbeth's possession of "all" indicates how Macbeth's fulfillment of the witches' prophecy at once represents the essence of tragic self-assertion, negatively defines the value of life, and positively implies a realm beyond tragedy. In fact, the fulfillment of the prophecy, as seen by Banquo, authenticates both the destructive view of tragedy and what will subsequently become the regenerative view of Shakespeare's romances. The "all" that Macbeth now possesses is tragic in a number of respects. For one thing, the titles themselves have a tragic legacy. As Thane of Glamis Macbeth lived in what he calls "blessed time" (III.iii.92), a period of time exempt from tragedy, but as Thane of Cawdor and King he inherits a legacy of tragic death. The earlier Thane of Cawdor, like Macbeth, was a traitor, and the King has been murdered. Indeed, one couplet at the end of I.ii captures the irreversible logic of Macbeth's tragic possession of "all." About the first Thane of Cawdor, the King says, "go pronounce his present death, / And with the former title greet Macbeth." The seeming value of the former title, its ostensible upward swing in Macbeth's career, is undercut by the rhyme that implies equivalence of "Macbeth" and "death."

Moreover, if we look at the second speech I have quoted, we can again see how the play's tragic action, built on Macbeth's attempts to possess and destroy "all," dramatizes the compressed, irreversible time of tragedy which moves toward an absolute close, at the same moment that it intimates what Banquo experiences, in an expanded version of time, as hope. Macduff's dirgelike assertion of "all" is indisputably a death knell. Nevertheless, even though the death of Macduff's family is tragic, that very tragedy continues to authenticate the period of hope intimated by Banquo's earlier speech. Macduff's line, "He has no children," expresses a tragic loss, but it also suggests the one possession which lifts Banquo's fate beyond tragedy; for he has children and they shall be kings. Again, the play's tragic action is defined against the witches' equivocal prophecy, and the diverse fates of the characters play on diverse understandings of time. That is, the short run of Macbeth's death, with which the play is primarily concerned, defines the longer run of Banquo's destiny which, though only intimated, represents a potential alternative to tragedy. Children, not titles, are the one possession—the one "all"—which can elevate individual destiny beyond tragedy.

The lack of children, on the other hand, traps Macbeth and Macduff within an exclusively tragic action.

The final speech in the series—Macbeth's "To-morrow, and to-morrow, and to-morrow"—at once forms the tragic answer to the "seeds of time" and demonstrates that Macbeth is not only the protagonist of a tragic play but a working definition of tragedy in action. Having tried to possess "all" by destroying "all," he defines his own action, as well as the action of tragedy, as "nothing." The tragic pathos of Macbeth's meditation on "to-morrow" is that his future, unlike Banquo's, is without hope. The irreversible logic of Macbeth's tragedy is such that he has no wife, no children, no to-morrow: just death. The absolute close of tragedy is precisely defined by Lady Macbeth: "What's done cannot be undone" (V.i.68). As Macbeth projects forward to tomorrow, he sees nothing but repetition and redundancy; there is nothing beyond, save his submission to oblivion. His vision is so constructed that not only is he the agent of tragedy, but he becomes the supreme spokesman of tragedy. He becomes the player who plays out the tragic version of life; he comes to view himself as the author and actor of his own tragedy. He is the idiot who tells his own tale, and whose words and actions serve to define the "nothing" which is tragic necessity.

In a manner reminiscent of *Macbeth*, *King Lear* is also a play that ultimately signifies the nothing which is tragedy. Throughout the first three acts, the tragic action of *King Lear* centers on diverse versions of nothing.[3] The basis of this preoccupation occurs in I.i when Lear turns to Cordelia, and asks,

> what can you say to draw
> A third more opulent than your sisters? Speak.
> *Cordelia.* Nothing my lord.
> *Lear.* Nothing?
> *Cordelia.* Nothing.
> *Lear.* Nothing will come of nothing, speak again. (I.i.85-90)

The sentence "Nothing will come of nothing" may well be a cryptic definition of tragedy, in which case Lear and Cordelia respectively express the beginning of tragedy and the attempt to prevent it, as we can see by examining their diverse uses of "nothing."

In calling for Cordelia to say something, Lear is in fact commanding her to use language destructively; and Goneril and Regan, in saying something, have exercised a form of language—characterized by Cordelia as "that glib and oily art / To speak and purpose not" (I.i.224-25)—which amounts to nothing, and which initiates the destructive forces of the play. By saying nothing Cordelia is affirming something of great value which could impede tragedy, and which intimates the language of romance. She tells Lear, "I love your majesty / According to my bond," and she subsequently defines that bond as returning "those duties back as are right fit, / Obey you, love you, and most honor you" (I.i.97-98). The tragic paradox is that Cordelia's virtual silence—her refusal to say something—constitutes an affirmation of a bond of value which is destroyed by the "nothings" that Lear demands and that Goneril and Regan gladly supply. This bond defines the legitimacy of natural, political, familial, and personal value in the play, and its violation stimulates a new disorder of illegitimacy and bastardy—a violent pattern of self-assertion—which becomes the tragic equivalent and dramatic embodiment of the phrase, "Nothing will come of nothing."

This new disorder of nothings elicited by Lear's command to his daughters appears throughout the first three acts of the play, and it is based on an inversion of value such that prior nothings become something, and prior somethings are debased to nothing. For example, in the very first lines of the play we are told that Lear had "more affected the Duke of Albany than Cornwall . . . but now in the division of the kingdom, it appears not which of the Dukes he values most." The act of arbitrary division, in other words, denies the hierarchical principle of value which distinguishes between the more and the less valuable, and between what is and is not tragic. Lear's instincts, as the play subsequently bears out, are correct: Albany is more valuable than Cornwall, but this judgment is destroyed until Act V by Lear's desire to level judgment, thereby enacting a horizontal principle of value, a flat scale of nothingness, that is wholly antithetical to the vertical order over which Lear, as king, presides. This desire to level and thereby collapse value leads Lear to quantify and objectify relationships which formerly were of intrinsic worth. Thus Cordelia, who like Albany is a favorite, is forced to regain, quantifiably, her original value by speaking "a third more opulent" than her sisters. By equalizing all value Lear has reduced people of value to nothing, just as he has enabled people of little or no value to become something by playing a numbers game. The difference between real value and the nothing which is numerical value is the difference between the King of France's estimate of Cordelia—"She is herself a dowry" (I.i.241)—and Lear's demand to have her speak "a third more opulent" to prove her worth.

This same perversion of value, which allows nothings to become something and diminishes somethings to nothing, also appears in the Gloucester plot. Edmund, who is illegitimate and hence nothing (he has no claim to his father's estate), becomes something by identifying Edgar, who is legitimate, with nothing. When he presents a forged letter to Gloucester, Edmund enacts and entraps Gloucester in another version of nothing:

> *Gloucester.* What paper were you reading?
> *Edmund.* Nothing, my lord.
> *Gloucester.* No? What needed then that terrible dispatch of it into your pocket? The quality of nothing hath not such need to hide itself. Let's see. Come, if it be nothing, I shall not need spectacles. (I.ii.30-35)

What Gloucester sees is a faked something which is nothing, offered by a nothing (a bastard) who presents himself as a something (a loyal son). Here, then, we see another version of how this tragedy is built on the idea that "nothing will come of nothing."

But we find the most comprehensive explanation of how the phrase "Nothing will come of nothing" sums up the first three acts of *King Lear,* as well as illumines the meaning of tragedy, when Lear and the Fool try to determine the meaning of nothing and how it applies to Lear himself. The Fool attempts to teach Lear a speech (I.iv.117-27) which enigmatically alludes to the need always to preserve something, lest you become nothing. Lear replies that the speech is "nothing," and the Fool responds:

> Then 'tis like the breath of an unfeed lawyer,
> you gave me nothing for't. Can you make no use
> of nothing, nuncle?
> *Lear.* Why no, boy, nothing can be made out of
> nothing. (129-33)

But the Fool does make something out of nothing by showing how Lear's divisive actions have destroyed his legitimacy and debased him, like Cordelia, Edgar, and Kent, to a kind of bastard: "Thou hast par'd thy wit o' both sides, and left nothing i' th' middle . . . now thou art an O without a figure. I am better than thou art now, I am a Fool, thou art nothing" (187-88, 192-94). The Fool clearly defines Lear as zero—an "O." Lear has both left nothing in the middle, meaning that his divisive actions have destroyed any ordering or validating principle of legitimacy, at the same time that Lear, as the tragic protagonist, is the "nothing" at the middle of the play, from which all further nothings devolve.

I have placed such a strong emphasis on the repeated use of "nothing" in the first three acts because, for all intents and purposes, these usages show how the three acts construct a tragedy which, to borrow from *Macbeth,* truly signifies nothing. It is as if the first three acts are a massive footnote to, and explanation of, Macbeth's locution; and by the end of Act III it looks as though this debased principle of disorder is about to exhaust itself. The main characters themselves begin to feel the exhaustion of tragedy and intimate a realm beyond tragedy. Lear himself expresses the antithesis to tragic disorder in a way that duplicates and validates Cordelia's earlier refusal to speak nothing: "I will be the pattern of all patience, / I will say nothing" (III.ii.37-38). The "pattern of all patience," in Shakespeare's romances, signifies a kind of resignation to, and exhaustion of, tragedy which precedes the entry of a realm of experience beyond tragedy. This swing from tragedy to romance is evident in the conjunction of the terrible blinding of Gloucester at the end of Act III and Edgar's opening speech in Act IV, which intimates the regenerative powers of romance:

> Yet better thus, and known to be contemn'd,
> Than still contemn'd and flatter'd. To be worst,
> The lowest and most dejected thing of fortune,
> Stands still in esperance, lives not in fear.
> The lamentable change is from the best,
> The worst returns to laughter. Welcome then,
> Thou unsubstantial air that I embrace. (IV.i.1-7)

This desire or possibility of transforming tragedy into an intimation of romance appears in a number of ways throughout Act IV.[4] For one thing, Lear and Cordelia, as well as Gloucester and Edgar, are reunited; the legitimacy of paternity is restored. Similarly, for the first time the "right" people are either destroyed (Cornwall and Oswald) or revealed to be the traitors they are (Goneril, Regan, and Edmund). The disorder of nothings begins to consume itself. Moreover, a number of characters continually attempt to invoke beneficent providential powers, whose entry is so vital to Shakespeare's romances. The last line of Act III is "Now heaven help him [Gloucester]!" and this invocation, although it is finally frustrated, intimates the need for hierophany which is characteristic of romance. Albany first states the need for heavenly intervention:

> If that the heavens do not their visible spirits
> Send quickly down to tame these vild offenses,
> It will come,
> Humanity must perforce prey on itself,
> Like monsters of the deep. (IV.ii.46-50)

Shortly thereafter, a messenger announces Cornwall's death and Albany clearly believes the "visible spirits" of heaven have intervened: "This shows you are above, / You justicers" (78-79). And Cordelia, too, invokes the gods to heal her father: "O you kind gods! / Cure this great breach in his abused nature" (IV.vii.13-14).

What happens throughout Act IV, then, is that Edgar and Cordelia, in particular, attempt to invoke and create a sense of the miraculous which is an attribute of romance. They attempt to reverse tragic time, to open up an apparent absolute close by submitting to providential necessity, and to affirm the value which has been negated in the first three acts. Nevertheless, though they define their romance actions against tragedy, these actions occur within the framework of a tragedy; and this tension between tragedy and romance is visibly displayed in the last two scenes of Act IV and in the opening scenes of Act V.

The famous Cliffs of Dover scene in Act IV.vi represents Edgar's attempt to show how a sense of the miraculous may grow out of the worst of misery. In this scene Edgar tries to convince Gloucester that tragedy isn't necessarily the be-all and end-all, that there is a realm of experience beyond tragedy which is dependent on acts of faith and patience. The "extreme verge," to which Edgar refers (IV.vi.26), is not only the cliff but the separation between the absolute close of tragedy and an entrance into a realm of recovery beyond tragedy. Thus when Gloucester "jumps," Edgar intends to dramatize the exhaustion of tragedy through Gloucester's apparent survival. The "fall," customarily associated with tragedy, is transformed by a deliberate enactment of ostensible miracle. In his attempt to dramatize a version of romance, Edgar tells Gloucester, "Thy life's a miracle" (55) and "therefore, thou happy father, / Think that the clearest gods, who make them honors / Of men's impossibilities, have preserved thee" (72-74). Edgar pleads that because tragedy has been reversed, Gloucester should now "Bear free and patient thoughts" (80).

In the same way Cordelia, too, attempts to lift Lear beyond the realm of tragedy by suggesting that the tragic action has been exhausted. The whole of IV.vii, like IV.vi, is suffused with a sense of penitence, forgiveness, and salvation. Lear believes himself to have been lifted "out o' th' grave" (IV.vii.44), paralleling Gloucester's earlier experience; he thinks Cordelia is "a soul in bliss" (45) and a "spirit"; and Cordelia asks Lear to "look upon me, sir / And hold your hand in benediction o'er me" (56-57). Finally, the Doctor argues, again suggesting the exhaustion of tragedy, that "the great rage, / You see, is killed in him" (78-79), and Lear's last words to Cordelia, before he leaves, seem to confirm their survival of tragedy: "Pray you now forget, and forgive" (84). These two scenes have absolute equivalents in Shakespeare's romances; indeed, in action and vocabulary they are characteristic of the conclusions to the romances. But the point, and it is a fatal point, is that these two scenes occur in Act IV, not Act V, and thus they only intimate an alternative which is utterly destroyed at the end of Act V.

Even as late as V.iii Lear, now imprisoned with Cordelia, continues Edgar's and Cordelia's attempts to lift the play beyond tragedy. Though imprisoned, Lear argues that he and Cordelia are free of a tragic world and thereby endowed with a kind of divine awareness. They are, he declares, above it all, the inhabitants of a realm beyond tragedy:

> We two alone will sing like birds i' th' cage;
> When thou dost ask me blessing, I'll kneel down
> And ask of thee forgiveness. So we'll live,
> And pray, and sing, and tell old tales, and laugh
> At gilded butterflies, and hear poor rogues
> Talk of court news; and we'll talk with them too—
> Who loses and who wins: who's in, who's out—
> And take upon's the mystery of things
> As if we were God's spies. (V.iii.9-17)

But Shakespeare is again tantalizing the audience with an alternative which is consumed. For the "mystery of things" is wholly dependent on Lear's continued reunion with Cordelia; only together can they act as "God's spies." Yet the clear purpose of this intimated alternative, as it may be the purpose of Act IV, is to push this play toward a version of tragedy which will "top extremity" (V.iii.208). In this respect, William Matchett is quite correct in observing: "Every time Shakespeare raises our hopes, he pulls the rug out from under us. This is the rhythm of *King Lear,* and it remains consistently so to the end of the play."[5]

For example, the survivors, who normally impose order at the end of Shakespeare's tragedies, are apparently disoriented and despairing at the end of the play. Albany wants Kent and Edgar to "Rule in this realm and the gored state sustain" (V.iii.321), again tragically dividing a kingdom that yearns for stability, but Kent declines, implying that he is soon to die; and Edgar never specifically answers Albany's request: "The weight of this sad time we must obey, / Speak what we feel, not what we ought to say" (324-25).[6] What Edgar feels is despair; what he ought to say is "yes." What he yields to, understandably, is not a sense of duty, but rather the "weight"—the destructive impact—of tragic time. Unlike Shakespeare's other tragedies, where as in *Macbeth* a tragic action exhausts itself in order to create a new, free time, *King Lear* also exhausts the basis of that "free" time by completely destroying its own intimations of romance; this is the significance and tragic necessity of Cordelia's death. Macbeth's death authenticates a prophecy of new time, with Banquo's sons symbolizing a realm beyond tragedy. Lear—the man and the play—appropriately leaves us with nothing.

Unlike *Macbeth* and *King Lear, Antony and Cleopatra* systematically displays an alternative to its tragic action. In a sense *Antony and Cleopatra* has it both ways—tragedy and tentative romance—and this is what makes the play at best a problematical tragedy.

As many people have noted, the play is built on a cumulative series of paradoxes which are not just stylistic conceits but antithetical conceptions of the "world." All of these paradoxes, in which loss from one point of view is gain from another, derive from the general comparison of Roman and Alexandrian views of life—both its purpose and its value.[7] If we take the various characteristics of Shakespearean tragedy—the dramatization of "boundary situations," the tension between self-assertion and submission, the affirmation of value through tragic negation, the use of irreversible time, and the turn toward an absolute close—and apply them to this play, we see that Antony is the stage, so to say, on which Caesar and Cleopatra conduct a tug of war between tragedy and romance.

Toward the end of Act II, Caesar and Antony are on board Pompey's galley, and Pompey, as well as Antony, is anxious to turn the gathering into a drunken Alexandrian feast. Caesar, however, objects to the revelry, and in response to Antony's suggestion that he become "a child o' th' time" Caesar replies, "Possess it, I'll make answer" (II.vii.100-101). This brief exchange concerning how to use time is just one of a number of instances where diverse understandings of time are expressed which intimate the antithetical views of Roman tragedy and Alexandrian romance. The Roman view of time, which is essentially tragic, upholds the value of individual accomplishment and asserts, by acts of possession, the values of moral responsibility and political power. The Alexandrian view, to the contrary, argues that man does not possess time; rather he is a "child" of it, which is to say he is subject to, rather than master of, time.[8] Because it is much less assertive and ambitious, the Alexandrian view correspondingly trivializes the value of public achievements, on which the magnitude of tragedy is based, and is far less preoccupied with moral responsibility and the acquisition of political power. Now I am not saying that at this point Antony is wholly committed to an Alexandrian view, nor am I trying to provide an overly ingenious reading of Antony's defense of drunkenness. But if we look back for a moment to earlier parts of the play, we can see that Antony's and Caesar's brief exchange illuminates the antithetical views of time associated with tragedy and romance.

In almost call-and-response fashion Acts I and II eddy back and forth between Alexandrian and Roman views of time, just as the scenes move back and forth between Rome and Alexandria. Antony states both views of time, because for the first three acts he straddles the two worlds; but Cleopatra's and Caesar's understanding of time never wavers. Adopting the Alexandrian view, Antony says to Cleopatra:

> Let's not confound the time with conference harsh;
> There's not a minute of our lives should stretch
> Without some pleasure now. What sport to-night?
>
> (I.i.45-47)

Later Cleopatra asserts a similar view when she tries to keep Antony from returning to Rome:

> When you sued staying,
> Then was the time for words; no going then;
> Eternity was in our lips and eyes,
> Bliss in our brows' bent, none our parts so poor
> But was a race of heaven. (I.iii.33-37)

Furthermore, Cleopatra defines time exclusively in terms of Antony's absence and presence; thus she takes mandragora while Antony is away so that she "might sleep out this great gap of time / My Antony is away" (I.v.5-6). She also defines her own color as an example of how she is a fully immersed child of the time: "Think on me, / That am with Phoebus' amorous pinches black, / And wrinkled deep in time?" (I.v.27-29). Her visual appearance carries with it, throughout the play, a legacy of eternal time (she has outlived several Roman rulers) antithetical to Caesar's present desires for worldly possession.

The Roman view of time, not surprisingly, is precisely the opposite of Alexandrian expectations. Its claims are wholly public; its values continually refer to public service, power, and duty. Antony himself, on leaving Cleopatra, tries to accommodate both views:

> Hear me, Queen:
> The strong necessity of time commands
> Our services awhile; but my full heart
> Remains in use with you. (I.iii.41-44)

Here Antony appears to be pledging his body to Roman service and his heart to Cleopatra. But the Roman view, like the Alexandrian, does not allow for divided loyalties; it is just as emphatic in its claims for the proper use of time and affirmation of public value. Caesar's condemnation of Antony, and hence of Alexandrian time, is absolute:

> yet must Antony
> No way excuse his foils, when we do bear
> So great weight in his lightness. If he fill'd
> His vacancy with his voluptuousness,
> Full surfeits and the dryness of his bones
> Call on him for't. But to confound such time
> That drums him from his sport and speaks as loud
> As his own state and ours, 'tis to be chid—
> As we rate boys who, being mature in knowledge,
> Pawn their experience to their present pleasure,
> And so rebel to judgment. (I.iv.23-33)

We get more than a glimpse of Roman uses of time, and of the Roman exercise of judgment, when Agrippa, with Caesar's approval, suggests the purely political feasibility of arranging the marriage between Antony and Octavia. Agrippa's plan does not arise from the spur of the moment; rather in true Roman fashion it is a "studied, not a present thought, / By duty ruminated" (II.ii.37-38). Typically, the Romans are always associated with "studied" thoughts—with the controlled exercise of reason which is their primary duty—and the Alexandrians, from the Roman perspective, are forever enmeshed in "present pleasures"—impulsive experiences rather than prudent acts of assertion and possession. This opposition is so absolute that Shakespeare dramatizes two antithetical versions of the same sentence, both referring to Antony. Comparing his own responsible use of time with Antony's irresponsible pleasures, Caesar says, "Yet must Antony / No way excuse his foils when we do bear / So great weight in his lightness." But where Caesar bears the heavy weight of responsibility, Cleopatra laments the loss of another weight: "O happy horse, to bear the weight of Antony!" (I.v.21).

I have looked briefly at the contrasting uses of time in the play and the way they define acts of self-assertion. Now let us examine two other characteristics of Shakespearean tragedy: the value placed on individual life and the turn toward an absolute close. In a successful tragedy, the tragic protagonists themselves value their own lives and thus, by implication, the continuation of human life itself. By the end of Act IV, when Antony is dead, Caesar clearly possesses the earth—he is the sole ruler of the world. The only thing left for him to acquire is Cleopatra, so that he can march her through the streets of Rome in celebration of his total victory. If, however, we compare Caesar's response to Antony's death with Antony's response to his own death, we demonstrably arrive at two antithetical interpretations of individual life—the one full of tragic expectations, the other just as fully denying those expectations.

Hearing of Antony's death, Caesar tragically exclaims:

> The breaking of so great a thing should make
> A greater crack. The round world
> Should have shook lions into civil streets,
> And citizens to their dens. The death of Antony
> Is not a single doom, in the name lay
> A moi'ty of the world. (V.i.14-19)

Were Antony's death tragic, all of Caesar's "shoulds" should have taken effect. For Caesar's estimation of the world—both its possession and its loss—is entirely tragic. But the "crack" Caesar expects does not produce a bang, nor even a whimper. In his death speech Antony explicitly denies all tragic expectations, telling the characters, as well as the audience, "The miserable change now at my end / Lament nor sorrow at" (IV.xv.51-52). Caesar, it appears, is presumptuously, though understandably, imposing a tragic view on a protagonist who denies he is a figure of tragedy.

The question is, if Antony's death is not tragic, what is it? I think Act IV implies two versions of an answer, the one affirmatively, the other negatively. The affirmative answer occurs, paradoxically, when Antony commits suicide; instead of lamenting his own need to die, he exclaims:

> but I will be
> A bridegroom in my death, and run into't
> As to a lover's bed. (IV.xiv.99-101)

Cleopatra, when she dies, takes these words right out of Antony's mouth: "Husband, I come!" (V.ii.287), suggesting not only a spiritual destination, but an act of sexual consummation. The suggestion is that Antony, although he dies, has in fact escaped tragedy and expects to be reunited with Cleopatra as a bridegroom, in a realm beyond tragedy which is at once spiritual and sensual. Cleopatra supplies the negative answer to the question when, watching Antony die, she estimates the value of Antony and the world:

> Shall I abide
> In this dull world, which in thy absence is
> No better than a sty? O, see, my women:
> The crown o' th' earth doth melt. (IV.xv.60-63)

Here Cleopatra echoes Antony's much earlier lines, "Let Rome in Tiber melt, and the wide arch / Of the ranged Empire fall!" (I.i,33-34), as if Antony's death has now fulfilled a prophecy and validated an authentic escape from tragedy. This alternative to tragedy is based on a contemptuous interpretation of Caesar's tragic understanding of the "world" and its value. From Caesar's point of view, the fall of empires should be tragic because it defines the magnitude of human life; yet what Caesar values, from Cleopatra's standpoint, is inconsequential, something "no better than a sty."

Moreover, one should not overlook the structural position of Antony's supposedly tragic death. To put it simply, tragic protagonists ordinarily do not die at the end of the fourth act. What is Act V supposed to do? My answer is just as simple as the question. Act V repudiates tragedy, and in doing so alludes to a romance alternative. At the end of Act IV, Cleopatra plans a suicide "after the high Roman fashion," to be accomplished in "the briefest end." But she clearly rejects this intention, which would have conformed with Roman expectations of tragedy. It is fascinating to watch how in Act V she taunts Caesar, frustrating his acquisitive impulses, and reversing the absolute close of tragedy which Caesar believes to be irreversible. Cleopatra thus opens up a view of another world beyond tragedy—a world which is calculated to test the audience's sense of faith (in a nonreligious sense) and threshold of feeling. To the extent that the audience is persuaded by and committed to Caesar's rational, though tragic, view, Cleopatra's alternative, like Antony's suicide, is no alternative at all. Rather, it is pure delusion. But if the audience is capable both of imagining and experiencing nonrational alternatives, then Cleopatra's choice at once diminishes the possibility of tragedy and affirms a view of life which will become the central experience of Shakespearean romance.

Cleopatra expresses this alternative to tragedy in two ways: first when she presents her convictions in the form of a dream to the characteristically skeptical Roman, Dolabella; and second, when she publicly authenticates her conviction by committing suicide. Cleopatra tells Dolabella that she "dreamt there was an Emperor Antony" (V.ii,76)—clearly an emperor of some other nonearthly world—and that

> His legs bestrid the ocean, his rear'd arm
> Crested the world, his voice was propertied
> As all the tuned spheres, and that to friends;
>
> .   .   .   .
>
>   For his bounty,
> There was no winter in't; an autumn it was
> That grew the more by reaping. His delights
> Were dolphin-like, they show'd his back above
> The element they liv'd in. (82-84, 86-90)

This dream enacts a moment where the play, from Cleopatra's point of view, defies the irreversible, male-dominated logic of tragedy, offering the audience an alternative which can only appear as a dream so long as it is construed within the conventions and expectations of Caesarian rationality. The authenticity of the dream can only be affirmed, that is, by negating or exceeding the conventional boundaries of tragedy. The tragic view estimates the size and value of the world exclusively in terms of physical existence—its loss or continuation. But Cleopatra affirms her romance alternative, first through the report of her dream and then through her suicide, which is designed to frustrate Caesar's tragic expectations.

Listen, for example, to Cleopatra's speech as she dresses up for death:

> Give me my robe, put on my crown, I have
> Immortal longings in me. . . .
>   Methinks I hear
> Antony call; I see him rouse himself
> To praise my noble act. I hear him mock
> The luck of Caesar, which the gods give men
> To excuse their after wrath. Husband, I come!
> Now to that name my courage prove my title!
> I am fire and air; my other elements
> I give to baser life. (V.ii.280-81, 283-90)

If we do not have a romance hierophany here, we at least have it intimated in Cleopatra's "immortal longings." If Cleopatra does not physically hear a call, she at least has the strength of conviction, the faith, to answer it through death. Moreover, if Cleopatra is now "fire and air"—beyond the earth's pull—she not only bequeaths the tragic elements of earth and water to Caesar, which elements have been the stage of Caesar's conquests, but she mocks them as well. This is an extremely curious tragic denouement. For just as Caesar views the deaths of Antony and Cleopatra as tragic, so they view his survival as tragic. Caesar is, as Cleopatra earlier addresses him, "Sole sir o' th' world" (V.ii.120), but she also says that "'Tis paltry to be Caesar" (2), and that his world "is not worth leave-taking" (298). Indeed, she wishes that the asp, the instrument of her death, could speak so "That I might hear thee call great Caesar ass / Unpolicied!" (307-8).

For my purposes, the most interesting line in the last scene, the one which best suggests how the Alexandrian view defies the Roman tragic view, is spoken by a Roman guard who, when he sees the dead Cleopatra, exclaims: "All's not well; Caesar's beguil'd"

(V.ii.323). The guard does not lament the death of Cleopatra; he laments Caesar's loss—his inability to possess Cleopatra. "All's not well" in the sense that Caesar has lost the ultimate symbol of what he values. We should recall that earlier in Act V Caesar is fearful of being defeated by Cleopatra's death; he cautions Proculeius,

> Give her what comforts
> The quality of her passion shall require,
> Lest in her greatness, by some mortal stroke
> She do defeat us; for her life in Rome
> Would be eternal in our triumph. (V.i.62-66)

So there is ample precedent for construing Cleopatra's death as the defeat—Caesar's word—of Caesar. No less interesting and unusual, the play closes with all the Romans, including Caesar, trying to figure out *how* Cleopatra died—a problem they can rationally solve—but they don't understand *why* she died. Indeed, Caesar's closing speech continues to insist on a tragic conclusion, as if he were trying, by projection, to recoup *his* losses:

> High events as these
> Strike those that make them; and their story is
> No less in pity than his glory which
> Brought them to be lamented. (V.ii.60-63)

But Caesar's imposition of a tragic conclusion, whose boundaries he understands and expects, is entirely irrelevant from an Alexandrian standpoint. Because Caesar believes in the magnitude of public persons and political action (e.g. "See / High order in this great solemnity"), he necessarily construes the deaths of Antony and Cleopatra as tragic. But Antony and Cleopatra, at the point of greatest tragedy in Caesar's eyes, repudiate Caesar's expectations and affirm in death their confidence in a world beyond Caesar's tragic understanding. Thus the fall of Antony and Cleopatra is tragic only to the extent that we share Caesar's assumptions about time, the importance of public acts of self-assertion, the value of individual life, and the worth of worldly possessions. If we do not share Caesar's view, as Antony and Cleopatra finally do not, then we are left in the peculiar position, as Caesar is, of applying a tragic view to two seemingly tragic characters who, in fact, disclaim every attribute of tragedy, including death. In which case the Roman guard is absolutely right; all's not well because Caesar, like tragedy, has been "beguiled" by an Alexandrian romance.

THREE

Pericles and
the Conventions
of Romance

Pericles is a magnificent outline of the conventions of romance. Although there continue to be disputes about the authorship of the play—the predominant view being that Shakespeare wrote only the last three acts—this argument in no way affects my approach.[1] We know that Shakespeare had a major hand in the creation of the play, and we can therefore conclude that he was aware of the play's basic design and use of a variety of dramatic conventions. I must say, however, that the play's use of romance conventions is internally so consistent that I find it difficult, on purely sytlistic grounds, to be persuaded of the dual authorship view. Besides, the text of the play is in such bad repair that it is hard to see how one could assign, with much confidence, one scene or passage to Shakespeare and another to some anonymous author. There just does not appear to be a convincing basis for stylistic comparisons, especially if Shakespeare were working with a new mode of drama.

But textual matters aside, my basic point is this: *Pericles* is a skeletal romance, one in which all the conventions of romance are displayed though rarely individuated. The play, indeed, is a pure romance in the sense that it performs all the appropriate gestures of romance without inspecting, questioning, or qualifying them as *Cymbeline,* for example, does. The play may be viewed as a kind of first draft of the more complicated romances to follow, but it is no less valuable for its sketchy quality because it provides us with an opportunity to see the conventions of romance at work in an uncomplicated and completely affirmative form.[2]

In the last chapter we saw how various intimations of romance are negatively defined against the backdrop of tragedy. There is no question that in *Macbeth* and *King Lear* tragedy is the dominant dramatic framework, though I have argued that the Alexandrian view in *Antony and Cleopatra* represents a genuine and fully developed alternative to the Roman tragic view of life. Nevertheless, the Alexandrian view takes us only to the doorstep, as it were, of romance. Like Edgar and Cordelia in *King Lear,* Cleopatra tries to impose a romance view on tragic materials, but such an act of self-assertion implies that individuals can manufacture romance, whereas the experience of romance, as we shall see in *Pericles,* depends on an external intervention of providential powers, which at once incorporates individual initiatives and affirms the larger creative processes associated with the expansive time of romance. Lady Macbeth states the tragic view of time precisely when she says, "What's done cannot be undone." Yet it is important to realize that though romance enacts an experiential realm beyond tragedy, it does not achieve this level of experience as a result of the attempts of individuals to undo, in the manner of Cleopatra, what has been done in tragedy. On the contrary, the undoing of tragedy by romance in order to proceed beyond tragedy is accomplished through an expansive use and experience of time, and it is only as individuals submit to time, adopting an attitude of patience, that seemingly tragic consequences are reversed.

One need only compare, for example, Antony's advice "Be a child o' th' time" (II.vii.100) with another version in *Pericles,* whose meaning no longer depends on the antithetical presence of the Caesarian view of time:

> Whereby I see that Time's the King of men,
> He's both their parent, and he is their grave,
> And gives them what he will, not what they crave.
>   (II.iii.45-47)

Antony's statement asserts an abandonment to present pleasure and subsequently implies contempt for Caesar's studied possession of the public world. But Pericles's perception does not establish its meaning negatively; it is not defined against some other external threat or antithetical principle. Rather, his statement affirms a view of time which is characteristic of romance and dominates the entire play. In capsule form, Pericles's lines isolate several romance conventions which determine the action of the play.

From the premise that "Time's the king of men" (an assumption expressed also at the beginning of Act IV in *The Winter's Tale*) several things follow. First, the experience of time, not the possession of it, is a central feature of romance. One does not undo time in romance; one waits it out, patiently. Second, if time is the king of men, then individuals are subsidiary to the movement of time which means that the value of human activity and assertion, on which tragedy depends, is correspondingly diminished. This explains the curiously passive and quiescent qualities of Pericles himself, and later of Marina as well, who, in a Penelope-like manner, can "Sing, weave, sew, and dance" (IV.vi.183). One neither wastes time in idleness, as Caesar thinks Antony does, nor does one possess it, as Caesar wishes. Rather, in romance, one affirms his or her place in time by subjecting oneself to its processes, and this act of resignation, even as it diminishes individual initiative, is a gesture of faith in the beneficent processes of time.

Furthermore, what differentiates the romantic understanding and experience of time from the tragic one is the awareness that time is *both* man's "parent" and his "grave." Tragedy, in its use of irreversible time, continually insists on and dramatizes the fact that time is a grave, an absolute close. But romance displays the entire cycle of birth and death, and it thus proceeds beyond tragedy by showing how life emerges from death, and hence how the closed view of tragic time may be reversed in romance. One example of this entire cycle in romance occurs when Thaisa is thought to have died at Marina's birth. Out of apparent death, the absolute close of tragedy, emerges life: Marina is "this piece / Of your dead queen. . . . this fresh, new sea-farer" (III.i.17-18, 41). A similar scene occurs in III.ii when Cerimon brings Thaisa back to life; and it is interesting to see how Cerimon's life-affirming action is not taken as an individual accomplishment so much as it is construed as evidence of providential intervention: "The heavens, / Through you, increase our wonder" (III.ii.95-96). As we shall see later, characters throughout this play are viewed as either instruments or manifestations of providence; they are rarely, if ever, mimetically individuated.

Moreover, if time—that is, the expansive time of the cycle of birth and death—is the controlling power of Shakespeare's romances, then individuals are clearly time's subjects, not its masters. Time gives men "what he will, not what they crave," which simply means that even as individual actions are subsidiary to the larger processes of time, so individuals themselves achieve and affirm their own value by enduring, not controlling, the diverse movements of time. This is a very special form of endurance, a version of patience which should not be construed negatively as an equivalent to tragic victimization or exhaustion. In *King Lear* Edgar asserts an essentially tragic version of endurance when he counsels Gloucester: "Men must endure / Their going hence even as their coming hither, / Ripeness is all" (V.ii.9-11). Edgar is talking about enduring agony and, ultimately, death. The "ripeness" to which he refers is primarily the preparation for and imminence of a tragic fall. But because romance deals with the entire cycle of life and death, its version of "ripeness" is characteristically a movement from death to life, and its version of endurance is not like Kent's final estimate of Lear's death: "The wonder is he hath endured so long, / He but usurp'd his life" (V.iii.317-18). Rather the endurance of romance represents the ability to go through the entire life cycle of life and death, to experience a movement from death to life, which culminates, for example, in Pericles's reunion with his daughter. Such a moment defines the ability to endure beyond tragedy:

> Tell thy story;
> If thine, considered, prove the thousandth part
> Of my endurance, thou art a man, and I

Have suffered like a girl. Yet thou dost look
Like Patience gazing on kings' graves, and smiling
Extremity out of act. (V.i.134-39)

Marina is not construed as an individual so much as she becomes
the symbolic presence and affirmation of "Patience." Nor is Pericles's reunion with Marina seen exclusively as an act of individual
endurance so much as it becomes a symbolic representation of how
Patience, in "smiling / Extremity out of act," which is exactly
what romance does to the extremity of tragedy, can bring Pericles
back to life, in the sense that the extremity of his tragedy is a necessary preparation for the emergence of the joy and wonder that is romance.[3]

When Gower says that Pericles "bears / A tempest, which his
mortal vessel tears, / And yet he rides it out" (IV.iv.29-31), he is alluding to the movement of *Pericles* toward the romance realm beyond tragedy. What is especially revealing about these lines is their
conjunction of external, internal, and symbolic usages; for as Douglas Peterson has aptly remarked, "*Pericles* is a dramatic elaboration
on the tempest emblem and its variants."[4] I have previously mentioned the absorptive capacity of the romances; in these lines we can
see the underlying design of how these absorptive processes work.
Externally, Pericles bears a tempest in the sense that he is quite literally moved about by storms on the sea. These tempests, like time,
alternately function as a parent and as a grave. They separate Pericles from his loved ones, and they eventually reunite him with his
family. At the same time, the external forces of tempests on the sea
are also the occasion for, and point to, Pericles's internal tempest:
the sufferings not only of his body, but of his mind. Very much as
The Tempest does, though in a much less individuated manner, *Pericles* uses the external event of a tempest as a backdrop for mental experiences whch are the approximate equivalent of tragedy. Like
Prospero, Pericles suffers a psychological tempest, but unlike Lear,
whose "mortal vessel" is also torn by a tempest, both Prospero and
Pericles "ride it out." It is this ability to ride out a tempest, in all its

diverse meanings, that contributes to the romances' unique experience beyond tragedy.

The idea of riding out a storm is an apt, if obvious, metaphor for the design of romance. In tragedy, storms often signify the death of individuals, but in romance such storms are a prerequisite for survival. Moreover, tempests are the result of natural forces, not individual actions, and thus the attitude of patience and endurance in the romances is a gesture of one's understanding of, and resignation to, forces beyond human control. In a sense, the attitude of patience and endurance is less an individual decision than a symbolic gesture affirming one's place in the eternal order of the natural life cycle. The eternal substratum of the metaphor of riding out a tempest is, of course, the sea; for though the sea at once separates and reunites, kills and brings back to life, it is the one constant element underlying the cycle of life and death. Just as the sea is the natural symbol of time's eternity, so Gower acts as the human spokesman for the audience's understanding of time's eternal process.

At the beginning of the play Gower declares: "*Et bonum quo antiquius, eo melius*" ("and the older a good thing is, the better"). What is particularly fascinating about this formulation is that if we link it up with the earlier notion that "Time's the king of men" it looks as if the play's represented time of fourteen years does not lead forward so much as it proceeds backward, to the roots, of eternal time—in this case to the sea. This backward movement may be seen in the plot structure of *Pericles*. For example, a case could be made that Acts IV and V fold back on Acts I–III in such a way that the play's ostensible movement forward is as well a movement back to the ancient roots that Gower refers to. Fourteen years separate III.iv from Act IV, but this separation is not so much represented as it is dramatized by its absence. The absence of fourteen years, like the absence of sixteen years in *The Winter's Tale,* permits us to regard Acts IV and V as an alternate beginning and end to the beginning and end of Acts I–III. In fact, a number of scenes in Acts IV and V appear to be variations of scenes in the first three acts. In IV.i. Leonine is told to assassinate Marina, just as Thaliard in I.i is ordered to assassinate Pericles. The brothel scenes in Act IV draw on the colloquial and comic language of II.i, and just as Pericles is subjected to a test in Act II at the court of Simonides, where he gains a wife, so Marina is subjected to a test in the brothel at Mytilene, which test culminates in Lysimachus's desire to marry Marina (V.i.261ff.). Similarly, the tempestuous shipboard scene in III.i occurs in a new variation in V.i, and Cerimon's life-affirming activities in III.ii occur again in the concluding scene of the play at the temple of Diana.

The characters, as well, mirror this process of folding backward into ancient and eternal time, as we shall see shortly. As individuals they move through fourteen years of represented time, but they achieve a stable identity only to the extent that they are symbolically conjoined with eternal time, just as Marina becomes a figure of Patience "smiling extremity out of act." Gower's preoccupation with ancient time is identified with the reversible and absorptive time of romance, and I am thus unable to agree with Kenneth Semon's view that a tension exists in the play "between Gower's mechanical understanding of the actions as he presents them, and the fantastic events which defy such mechanical understanding."[5] Gower's preference for antique time makes him the spokesman for romance in the sense that the play, seen as an expression of his preferences, is not so much the movement forward toward change and progression one expects from realistic drama as it is a folding backward to what is stable, eternal, and primarily emblematic and archetypal. What this backward movement accomplishes, both in language and characterization, is two forms of absorption, whereby the play elicits a sense of eternal time beyond tragedy.

Just as the sea in the first four acts separates characters in a tragic version of a tempest, only to absorb these tragic separations in the fifth act, so the play's diverse uses of simile can be seen to reflect this process of separation and eventual absorption. Similes presume disjunction even as they represent attempts to enforce union, and in the fifth act the similes give way to a series of emphatic declarations of identity, which not only point to the reunion of characters, but signify the moment that eternal time is restored. Clearly one must be careful not to press this point too hard, since similes can perform different tasks and are the common currency of all Shakespearean drama. Nevertheless, the movement from "like" to "is" in *Pericles* seems to carry with it considerable emotional impact.[6]

From the first act until the beginning of Act V, the similes invariably point to human activities—both good and evil—and to the separation of individuals from providential processes. Any abbreviated list of these similes is, of course, both selective and biased, but the following examples are as representative a sampling as I can develop of their essentially formulaic uses. Pericles, on seeing Antiochus's daughter, says, "See where she comes, apparelled like the spring" (I.i.12), and Antiochus says of his own daughter, "Her face, like heaven, enticeth thee to view / Her countless glory, which desert must gain" (I.i.30-31). Here the similes elicit the conventional disjunction between exterior appearance and internal quality. Antiochus's daughter is a formulaic example of the alluring appearance of vice, and Pericles's initial perception of her is an equally conventional example of human misprision. Later, having translated the riddle alluding to incest, Pericles again reverts to similes which describe the conventional moral lesson to be gained by this event:

> How courtesy would seem to cover sin,
> When what is done is like an hypocrite,
> The which is good in nothing but in sight!
>
> .   .   .   .
>
> And both like serpents are, who though they feed
> On sweetest flowers, yet they poison breed.
>   (I.i.121-23, 132-33)

In I.iv we get the exact reverse of I.i. Whereas Pericles expected the best in Antioch and encountered the worst, in this scene Cleon and Dionyza expect the worst (they fear being conquered because of their country's starvation) only to experience Pericles's willingness to save them from destruction. Again the similes embody a conventional moral lesson—indeed, the dominant mode of discourse

throughout the play is moral aphorism[7]—with Cleon first expressing fear of evil only to have that fear dismissed by Pericles's charity:

> *Cleon.* Thou speaks't like [him's] untutored to repeat:
> What makes the fairest show means most deceit.
> (I.iv.74-75)

.   .   .   .

> *Pericles.* Let not our ships and number of our men
> Be like a beacon fir'd t' amaze your eyes.

.   .   .   .

> And these our ships, you happily may think
> Are like the Trojan Horse was stuff'd within
> With bloody veins, expecting overthrow,
> Are stor'd with corn to make your needy bread,
> And give them life whom hunger starv'd half dead.
> (I.iv.86-87, 92-96)

Similarly, in Act II the main function of the similes is both to assert,
by way of contrast with Antiochus's daughter, the genuine value of
Thaisa, who "Sits here like beauty's child, whom nature gat / For
men to see, and seeing wonder at" (II.i.6-7), and to affirm the real
virtue of princes, as opposed to the King of Antioch's vice:

> for princes are
> A model which heaven makes like to itself.
> As jewels lose their glory if neglected,
> So princes their renowns if not respected. (II.ii.10-13)

Appropriately, Thaisa adopts this formulaic mode of discourse, later
likening Pericles, another prince, to a jewel: "To me he seems like
diamond to glass" (II.iii.36).

Now I do not wish to belabor this point with further citation of
the similes' formulaic moral function, except to say that in Acts III
and IV similar usages of similes occur, all referring to distinctly human activities, to a sense of estrangement, and to the remoteness of
providential powers. Perhaps Pericles best characterizes the disjunc-

tions of the first four acts when he declares, "This world to me is a lasting storm, / Whirring me from my friends" (IV.i.19-20). The similes in the first four acts basically serve as a linguistic corollary to the tempestuous "Whirring" of fathers, wives, and daughters. In other words, the similes are both the vehicle and the linguistic equivalent of the characters' experience of potentially tragic separations.

On the other hand, the similes in Act V begin to hint at providential intrusions and the emergence of romance time. The distinctive language of romance, we begin to see, is the language of identity and of a nearly ineffable experience of harmony; only it is a peculiar form of identity which does not simply entail the rediscovery of apparently lost or dead individuals. The process of identity in romance is twofold, just as the cycle of life involves both birth and death. The first stage of identity is purely human; it restores the identification of lost individuals. The second and more important stage involve the merging of individuals with the eternal process of the life cycle itself, and this merging is brought about by the introduction of a hierophany. The hierophany is the ultimate nonhuman experience which makes all else possible, and which enables the characters to go beyond tragedy.

This twofold process may be seen in the linguistic design of Act V, which moves from analogy to identity to hierophany to Gower's concluding speech. The speech identifies all the central characters with emblems of the diverse experiences and human guises of eternal time. Early in Act V, for example, Marina is repeatedly likened to aspects of providence. She is so likened for two reasons: she is, as an individual, about as close as a human can be to the virtuous ways of providence; at the same time, however, she represents an estrangement from her roots, for "time hath rooted out my parentage" (V.i.92). Her "parentage," as we shall see, involves her reunion not only with her family, but with the healing processes of time itself. Seen as a symbol of eternal time, Marina "sings like one immortal, and she dances / As goddess-like to her admired lays" (V.Chorus.3-4). And when Pericles first sees her, he likens her, on a purely human level, to his wife—"My dearest wife was like this maid" (V.i.107), "thou lookest / Like one I lov'd indeed" (V.i.124-25)—and to the motions of providence:

> thou lookest
> Modest as Justice, and thou seemest a [palace]
> For the crown'd Truth to dwell in.

> Yet thou dost look
> Like Patience gazing on kings' graves. (V.i.119-21, 137-38)

Marina is at once human—a daughter—and a symbolic figure of Justice and the "crown'd Truth."

When Pericles finally does identify Marina, he does so in a way that recapitulates the various images of the sea and the tempest as forces of separation, transforming them into a providential experience which lifts the characters beyond tragedy:

> O Helicanus, strike me, honored sir,
> Give me a gash, put me to present pain,
> Lest this great sea of joys rushing upon me
> O'erbear the shores of my mortality,
> And drown me with their sweetness. O, come hither,
> Thou that beget'st him that did thee beget;
> Thou that was born at sea, buried at Tharsus,
> And found at sea again! O Helicanus,
> Down on thy knees; thank the holy gods as loud
> As thunder threatens us. This is Marina. (V.i.190-99)

This speech is a stunning summation of the conventions of romance. All the basic paradoxes of romance's movement beyond tragedy are embedded in the images, even as Pericles explicitly states the content of the experience of romance. The sea which separates ultimately rejoins; out of seeming death, life emerges; drowning is conjoined with sweetness, an early vision, perhaps, of *The Tempest*'s "sea-change," just as the sea "o'erbears" the shore of mortality, not to kill but to bring back to life. The identification of Marina emblematically affirms the beneficent powers of eternal time, and the appropriate human gesture is that of prayer, signifying the harmonious union between the gods and man that overcomes the disjunctions enacted by the play's similes.

Moreover, later in this scene Pericles experiences additional versions of a hierophany. He hears the music of the spheres (V.i.231-33), and when he falls asleep he has a vision of the goddess Diana who in telling him to go to Ephesus, the play's sacred ground, alludes to the basic formula of how romance proceeds beyond tragedy. She says to Pericles,

> Reveal how thou at sea didst lose thy wife.
> To mourn thy crosses, with thy daughter's, call
> And give them repetition to the [life]. (244-46)

The "repetition," to which she refers, is not merely a recital of what has occurred for fourteen years; it is a form of incantation in which the characters, like the language and structure of the play, gather up past separations to weld them into hierophanic identity. This incantatory recapitulation of the movement from likeness to identity is easily seen in Thaisa's reunion with Pericles:

> O my lord,
> Are you not Pericles? Like him you spake,
> Like him you are! Did you not name a tempest,
> A birth and death? (V.iii.31-34)

The play's prior separations and similes are repeated through recollection, but they are also absorbed into a moment of absolute union. "Like" becomes "are," death becomes new birth, and the tempest of romance is seen to be not the absolute and destructive close of tragedy, but the open and eternal cycle of life's renewal. Pericles says to Thaisa, "O come, be buried / A second time within these arms" (V.iii.43-44), and this is precisely, albeit paradoxically, what romance does: it creates a second time, a second "burial," which permits characters involved in error and misjudgment an opportunity once again to experience the fullness of life.

But there is an additional way, beyond the linguistic movement from analogy to identity, through which Act V structurally gives "repetition to the life." The second time that Pericles refers to, although it takes place in the present on the level of represented time, is as well a "burial" into the past—the past not just of the fourteen years before, but of the ancient time to which Gower had earlier referred. That is, the play is not resolved realistically at the level of character; it is resolved symbolically at the moment that providential powers intervene. In watching the characters move ostensibly through represented time, we have been observing, as Gower insists at the end of the play, the characters as motions and expressions of eternal time. Gower's concluding speech transforms the audience's sense of the characters as represented human beings into an experiential realm where character is not construed mimetically, but symbolically; and his concluding speech also serves as an interpretive paradigm of the play's use of romance conventions:

> In Antiochus and his daughter you have heard
> Of monstrous lust the due and just reward.
> In Pericles, his queen and daughter, seen,
> Although assail'd with fortune fierce and keen,
> Virtue [preserv'd] from fell destruction's blast,
> Led on by heaven, and crown'd with joy at last.
> In Helicanus may you well descry
> A figure of truth, of faith, of loyalty.
> In reverent Cerimon there well appears
> The worth that learned charity aye wears.
> For wicked Cleon and his wife. . . .
>
> .   .   .   .
>
> The gods for murder seemed so content
> To punish, although not done, but meant.
> So, on your patience ever more attending,
> New joy wait on you! Here our play has ending.
>   (V.iii.85-95, 99-102)

Taken as an interpretive paradigm of romance, Gower's speech insists on a kind of emblematic or figural consciousness, where characters are seen as symbolic figures of eternal truth.[8] His speech, moreover, suggests that the dominant activity of character in *Pericles* is one of ritualized gesture, where what you do is what you are. Psychology, the staple of character interpretation in realistic drama, gives way to a conception of character as diverse expressions of a single archetype—the place of human activity within the eternal cycle of life. Characters thus represent a spectrum of human activity, ranging from good to evil, but that spectrum is itself an inclusive image of eternal activity.

Interestingly, Gower's interpretation of character mirrors the play's stylistic movement from analogy to identity. As a poet, Gower would deal on a mimetic level with likeness, for all art, construed mimetically, is "like"—that is, an imitation of—some version of human experience. But in this last speech, Gower alters the concept of character from analogy, which functions at the level of represented time, to identity, a transformation which merges the characters with the movements of eternal time. That is, Antiochus and his daughter are not just like "monstrous lust"; they are individual embodiments of the eternal presence of lust, just as Cleon and Dionyza are eternal symbols of wickedness. Similarly, Pericles, Marina, Thaisa, Helicanus, and Cerimon are all identified with diverse aspects of those human activities which guide romance beyond tragedy and which function primarily at a symbolic level. Helicanus *is* a "figure of truth, of faith, of loyalty," Cerimon *is* a figure of "learned charity," as Prospero will be in *The Tempest,* and Pericles, Thaisa, and Marina *are* collective symbols of the providential experience of romance: through them we see "Virtue preserved from fell destruction's blast, / Led on by heaven, and crowned with joy at last."

Just as the characters are finally seen as emblems of eternity, so the entire play, as a romance, enacts the "new joy" which is the distinctive experience of romance. As Joan Hartwig has observed, "If the dramatic illusion has succeeded in its purpose, the members of the audience discover in themselves a potential for miracle."[9] However, that patience, though it dramatically appears as a forward movement through represented time, enacts a backward drift into eternal time. The "new joy" of romance is finally and firmly based on a harmonious merging with the antiquity of time, for, as Gower says, "*Et bonum quo antiquius eo melius.*" Romance, that is, is an ancient thing, and therefore better, because it goes back to eternal roots.

FOUR

Cymbeline
and the Parody
of Romance

If *Pericles* is an example of a pure romance, then *Cymbeline,* with its prominent emphasis on disjunction and mortality, is at once romance taken to its dramatic limits and a skeptical response to the optimism of *Pericles.* I have repeatedly emphasized the absorptive capacity of Shakespeare's romances—their ability to encompass diverse genres within a framework of reversible time—but in *Cymbeline* Shakespeare appears to test the absorptive capacity of romance, both generically and experientially, by overloading the structure of romance with seemingly recalcitrant details, characters, and experiences. It is almost as if Shakespeare set out to determine how much romance could successfully absorb without falling apart. Thus what is essentially formulaic in *Pericles* becomes problematical in *Cymbeline* because of Shakespeare's insistent, and frequently entertaining, experimentation.

Accordingly, *Cymbeline,* which Northrop Frye has aptly subtitled "Much Ado About Everything,"[1] stands in relation to the other romances in much the same way that *All's Well That Ends Well* and *Measure for Measure* relate to the other comedies. It is, if you will, a problem romance: we may cheerfully concede that *Cymbeline* employs many of the conventions we associate with romance, but at the same time we must acknowledge that the play extends those conventions to their limits, and possibly to their breaking point. In its use of time, character, and absorptive capacity the disjunctive world of *Cymbeline* wavers between tentative romance and pure parody, between wonder and laughter, between the expectation of providence and the experience of mortality.

To an extent, my own view of *Cymbeline* as a parody of romance has been influenced by some of Frank Kermode's observations. For example, Kermode argues that the tone of some scenes "is somehow suspiciously simple and open, as if Shakespeare were covertly parodying Fletcher," and Kermode also notices that the play's "last scene is hard to bring off on the stage because the too rigid untying of all those knots awakens farcical associations. (This is to assume that Shakespeare did not want it to)." The problem with Kermode's view is that he will allow for only intermittent, and sometimes inadvertent, parody, even though the play, as I intend to show, continually exploits the opportunity for parody. In the same way, F. D. Hoeniger pulls up short of the logical conclusion of his observations when he writes, "If *Cymbeline* is romance, then it is a romance of a kind that involves a highly ironic perspective towards the characters *up to close to the play's end* [my italics]." That highly ironic perspective toward the characters—or what Frye has called "the extraordinary blindness of the characters"[2]—in fact continues to the end of the play.

Bertrand Evans has convincingly demonstrated that *Cymbeline* is dominated by "discrepant awareness."[3] This sense of discrepancy appears throughout all the romances, though it is not unique to them. Pericles states the problem behind the conventional distinction between "inside" and "outside" when he observes, "How courtesy would seem to cover sin, / When what is done is like an hypocrite, / The which is good in nothing but in sight!" (I.i.121-23). The end toward which this formulation customarily develops in romance is expressed by the First Gentleman in *Cymbeline* when he says of Posthumus (in a characteristically mistaken estimation): "I do not think / So fair an outward and such stuff within / Endows a man but he" (I.i.22-24).[4] Similarly, on a structural level this movement from analogy to identity occurs, as in *Pericles,* when the play either folds back on itself or absorbs all past actions into a renewed and recapitulated present which is dependent on theophany.

What happens in *Cymbeline*, however, is that all the elements of absorption and romance reversal are present, but they never quite encompass or overcome the play's steady emphasis on discrepancy. The ideal of absorption is clearly stated when, for example, Imogen declares, "The dream's here still; even when I wake, it is / Without me, as within me; not imagined, felt" (IV.ii.306-7). But Imogen's assertion of faith in the role of Fidele is continually undercut—this very speech is spoken as she weeps over the headless body of Cloten, thinking it is Posthumus.

What I am suggesting is that *Cymbeline* is structurally a romance that experientially does not feel like one. It does not feel like one because the play, finally, is a parody of romance. The pleasure of the play derives from its ability to test and make fun of the very conventions of its own manner of proceeding. The audience is at once amazed, detached, and entertained by the incredible conclusion in V.v because it is less a resolution than a dramatic tour de force that parodies an expected romance resolution.

The three plots dealing with the King's separation of Posthumus and Imogen, the pastoral life of his two lost sons in Wales, and the external military threat from the Romans devolve from Cymbeline's diverse roles as father, husband, and king, and may be viewed, respectively, as outlines of the conventions of tragedy, pastoral romance, and history, with the play's conclusion serving as an example of romance absorption on a massive scale. Such a movement, as I shall show in the next chapter, does effectively occur in *The Winter's Tale*. But because the ostensible resolution of *Cymbeline* is partial, fragmentary, and hilarious—built as it is on a dazzling sequence of momentary revelations—the audience is made aware more of the play's labored fictional devices, somewhat akin to Jupiter's cranky version of theophany in V.iv, than of a sudden harmonious experience of eternal time. The Soothsayer, appropriately named Philharmonus, may wish us to believe that "The fingers of the pow'rs above do tune / The harmony of this peace" (V.v.466-67), but the audience, it seems to me, is more aware of his labored philological explication of the riddle. This is why I think it is essential to distinguish at the outset between the structure of the play—particularly its manipulation of romance conventions—and the audience's experience of the play. Because the play continually draws attention to its own exploitation of dramatic conventions, the audience remains superior to, detached from, but supremely entertained by what is finally a parody of romance.

A number of critics have wondered about the center of *Cymbeline* and what constitutes its major thematic concern. These ruminations, all of which concede a certain amount of bewilderment, have led to a variety of views, and their range is illustrated by the remarks of Norman Rabkin and Robert Grams Hunter. Having noticed the "ostentatious theatricality" of *Cymbeline,* Rabkin argues that

> only one explanation can account for what we have seen as a dominant element in the play: *Cymbeline* is a play as much about plays and play-making and play-going as it is about reconciliation. . . . Shakespeare's game is to engage us in the naive artifice of the piece, to make us believe in its reality, and then to make us recognize the game he is playing. . . . The world of tragedy can be redeemed in *Cymbeline,* as it could not in earlier Shakespearean tragedy, the play seems to say, simply because the playwright can deny its tragic inevitability by his power over the plot.[5]

Rabkin concludes that this is "an odd and perhaps disappointing theme; yet it seems to be the sum of what Shakespeare has to say in both *Pericles* and *Cymbeline.*"

If Rabkin sees the play as metatheater, an ongoing commentary on and experimentation with tragicomedy, Hunter argues that the play is essentially an enactment of Christian forgiveness. His interpretation places emphasis on Posthumus and Imogen, rather than on Shakespeare's artifice, and thus he argues that "the hero and the heroine share the significant action of the play between them, and in that sharing is a clue to Shakespeare's organization of the play's events."[6] Later Hunter concludes that "of the four romantic comedies of forgiveness, *Cymbeline* is the most overtly Christian, and it is in this Christianity, with the doctrines of repentance and regeneration at its center, that I would place that 'commanding significance, which penetrates the whole, ordering and informing everything,' which Dr. Leavis has denied to the play" (p. 176).

Now it is hard for me to see, or experience, Christian presence in a play whose presiding deity is Jupiter, and whose dramatic context is continually pagan.[7] Certainly repentance is the dominant note of the play's conclusion—Cymbeline officially declares, "Pardon's the word to all" (V.v.422)—but Christian doctrine has not cornered the market on a sense of repentance. Moreover, it is hard to detect the presence of regeneration. All the complications of the plot are resolved in V.v, but the characters are not so much changed and regenerated as they are reidentified and restored to their former status. Indeed, on either a psychological or a religious level the characters remain static—footnotes, as it were, to Philharmonus's explication of the riddle. They are literary explications of a text more than enactments of the experience of romance.

If we take the four characteristics of romance—the movement beyond tragedy unfolded against a seemingly tragic backdrop, the absorptive capacity, the use of reversible time, and the eventual presence of theophany—and test them against *Cymbeline,* I think we can see that the play is a genial parody, in which the romance conventions set up a disjunction between the characters' expectations of romance and their experience, as well as the audience's, of deflation, dispersal, and disorientation. In effect, Shakespeare uses all his dramatic resources to mimic and undermine the conventions of romance.

The various plots of the play, for example, all grow out of the ostensible experience or threat of tragedy. Curiously, in the First Folio *Cymbeline* appears as the last of the tragedies, for reasons that no one, myself included, can satisfactorily explain. As Rabkin has observed, if the play is a tragedy, it is a tragedy with a happy ending. Nevertheless, the three major plots are presented against a tragic backdrop. Cymbeline has broken up the marriage between Posthumus and Imogen and thereby lost the affection of his daughter and his remaining heirs. In fact, as Douglas Peterson has noted,[8]

some of the dialogue in I.i is occasionally reminiscent of Lear's condemnation of Cordelia, as when Cymbeline says to Imogen:

> O disloyal thing
> That shouldst repair my youth, thou heap'st
> A year's age on me.
> *Imogen.* I beseech you, sir,
> Harm not yourself with your vexation.
> I am senseless of your wrath; a touch more rare
> Subdues all pangs, all fears.
> *Cymbeline.*   Past grace? obedience?
> *Imogen.* Past hope, and in despair; that way past grace.
> (I.i.131-37)

Similarly, the consequence of this separation, involving Imogen,
Posthumus, and Iachimo, appears to be a duplication, as Rabkin has
observed, of the tragic story of Desdemona, Othello, and Iago—the
focus ostensibly being on an explicitly tragic failure of perception.

Still, the play's sense of tragedy can easily be overestimated. Iachimo is not so much a satanic Iago as he is a sneaky parody of Iago.
In the productions of *Cymbeline* that I have seen, the purportedly
malicious scene where Iachimo emerges from the trunk has invariably produced laughter—perhaps because the audience is less caught
up in Imogen's victimization than in Iachimo's scrupulous enumer-
ation of detail, down to the "mole cinque-spotted" (II.ii.38) on
Imogen's left breast. Iachimo is less a villain than an aesthete anat-
omist who almost lovingly mulls over detail. Moreover, when Iachimo files his report with Posthumus, observing, among other
things, that Imogen's breast is "(Worthy her pressing)" (II.iv.135),
such a scene may have the potential for tragedy, but Posthumus is
made to appear a fool rather than a tragic victim. His jealousy leads
him to a hyperbolic condemnation of women, somewhat reminiscent of Timon's railing against mankind—Posthumus says, "for
there's no motion / That tends to vice in man, but I affirm / It is
the woman's part" (II.v.20-22)—but the audience remains superior
to and detached from his ostensible tragedy. Posthumus is less a fig-

ure of tragedy—as, say, Leontes, will be in *The Winter's Tale*—than
he is an object of bemused contempt. He briefly goes through the
motions of tragedy, but he has been tricked, not just by Iachimo,
but by Shakespeare.

The other two plots—those involving Cymbeline's lost sons and
the impending war between Britain and Rome—also rely heavily
on the presence or emergence of apparent tragic loss. But again this
is only a convention which occasions the opportunity for parody.
To begin with, Shakespeare simply relates that the sons have been
lost for twenty years, and the matter is then dropped until III.iii.
Cymbeline is not preoccupied with this loss, in the way, for example, that Pericles continually refers to the loss of Thaisa and Marina,
nor does Imogen worry over the prolonged absence of her brothers.
Rather Shakespeare uses the lost sons, among other things, to parody the customary romance reunification of lost children. At the
very point, for instance, that Imogen and her brothers lament their
loss of one another, Shakespeare brings them, unknowingly, together. And the effect is not so much ironic as it is a delightful
spoof of another romance convention. When the lost brothers meet
their lost sister, disguised as Fidele, the parodic intent comes to the
surface:

> *Guiderius.*   Were you a woman, youth,
> I should woo hard but be your groom in honesty;
> I bid for you as I do buy.
> *Arviragus.*   I'll make't my comfort
> He is a man. I'll love him as my brother;
> And such a welcome as I'ld give to him
> After long absence, such is yours. Most welcome!
> Be sprightly, for you fall 'mongst friends.
> *Imogen.* [*aside*]   'Mongst friends?
> If brothers: Would it had been so, that they
> Had been my father's sons. . . . (III.vi.68-76)

Well, they are her father's sons; Imogen does not know it, but the
audience does. The repetition of "brothers," together with the allu-

sion to their twenty years' absence (e.g. "After long absence"), is just another characteristic instance where the conventions of romance are genially parodied. We will wait five acts, that is, for a romance reunion which occurs, temporarily, in the third act. Imogen and her brothers may feel a sense of loss, but that experience is swiftly dispelled for the audience.

The third plot, too, involves what might be called parodic retraction both for Cymbeline and for the Soothsayer, who is less in possession of than in search of "sooth." This is the only plot that, for a time in any event, might appeal to a British audience's sense of pride and patriotism. Cymbeline refuses to pay the customary tribute to the Romans, and in his refusal he occasions a fairly strong appeal to national pride. Even Cloten, who is the comic scapegoat of the other two plots, associated as he is with courtly ineptitude and rank body odor, is in this plot permitted to speak patriotically and to make fun of crooked Roman noses:

> There be many Caesars
> Ere such another Julius. Britain's a world
> By itself, and we will nothing pay
> For wearing our own noses. (III.i.11-14)

Of course, as Cloten speaks of noses Shakespeare may be parodically alluding to Cloten's smell: "Sir, I would advise you to shift a shirt; the violence of action hath made you reek as a sacrifice" (I.ii.1-2). But the promised combat between Rome and Britain, though we are told that it occurs, hardly plays a prominent part in the play; this plot is simply established to bring Iachimo, Posthumus, Imogen, Guiderius, Arviragus, and Belarius back, so that all the plots may eventually be resolved. In other words, the ostensible tragedy of this plot is much like the view of Cloten's death—"the fall of an ass, which is no great hurt" (I.ii.37)—and, interestingly, at the end of the play Cymbeline does pay the tribute, which I take as a parodic retraction.

In this plot the Soothsayer is also involved in a process of parodic retraction. With regard to romance conventions, the Soothsayer performs a role akin to the divine inspirations of romance. Like Pericles, for example, and Posthumus later in this play, he sees a vision on the eve of battle:

> Last night the very gods showed me a vision
> (I fast and pray'd for their intelligence) thus:
> I saw Jove's bird, the Roman eagle, wing'd
> From the spongy south to this part of the west,
> There vanished in the sunbeams; which portends
> (Unless my sins abuse my divination)
> Success to th' Roman host. (IV.ii.346-52)

It turns out that he is wrong, if by "Success" he means a Roman military victory. As with most events in the play, the Soothsayer's vision is characteristically "abused." But no matter; at the end of the play the Soothsayer, now less divinely inspired than determinedly ingenious, clarifies his prior vision:

> The vision
> Which I made known to Lucius, ere the stroke
> Of this yet scarce-cold battle, at this instant
> Is full accomplished; for the Roman eagle,
> From south to west on wing soaring aloft,
> Lessen'd herself, and in the beams o' th' sun
> So vanish'd; which foreshadow'd our princely eagle,
> Th' imperial Caesar, should again unite
> His favor with the radiant Cymbeline,
> Which shines here in the west. (V.v.467-76)

The war is really no war, the vision hardly accurate, just as the romance merely goes through the motions of romance.[9]

If we apply two other characteristics of romance—its absorptive capacity and its use of reversible time—we may again see how the play employs the customary gestures of romance only to parody them. The diverse plots of the play, as I suggested earlier, grow out of Cymbeline's various roles as father, husband, and king. The banishment of Posthumus and Imogen's departure to Wales constitute a potentially tragic plot which, in turn, occasions a second tragic plot, involving Imogen, Posthumus, and Iachimo. These plots are subsequently subdivided into pastoral romance, with Imogen temporarily though unknowingly reunited with her lost brothers in Wales, and history, as she is then moved into the plot with the Romans. Posthumus, on the other hand, moves from the domestic tragic plot, to the history plot, first as a nominal Roman and later as a British peasant. All these plots, including their subdivisions, are then absorbed in V.v, which presumably functions as the dramatic analogue to the romance experience that lifts the characters beyond tragedy. The structure of the play thus conforms with the romance principle of generic absorption.

Similarly, the principle of reversible time occurs within the play. Just as when Cymbeline twenty years earlier banished Morgan (now Belarius), he lost his two sons as a consequence, so when he banishes Posthumus he loses his remaining daughter and heir. In addition, Posthumus's desire to kill Imogen precipitates a parallel separation which, though spread over a much shorter period of time, sets up another opportunity for Shakespeare to reverse the seeming tragedy of the play. Moreover, in apparent anticipation of the expected reversal of tragedy which is the characteristic denouement of romance, Shakespeare dots the play with refrains, usually at the end of scenes, which allude to the end of tragedy and the advent of providential theophany:

> The heavens hold firm
> The walls of thy [Imogen's] dear honor; keep unshak'd
> That temple, thy fair mind, that thou mayst stand,
> T' enjoy thy banish'd lord and this great land! (II.i.62-65)

> May the gods
> Direct you [Imogen] to the best! (III.iv.192-93)

> Flow, flow,
> You heavenly blessings, on her [Imogen]! (III.v.160-61)

Be cheerful' wipe thine eyes;
Some falls are means the happier to arise. (IV.ii.402-3)

All other doubts, by time let them be clear'd,
Fortune brings in some boats that are not stear'd.
(IV.iii.45-46)

The time seems long, their blood thinks scorn
Till it fly out and show them princes born. (IV.iv.53-54)

In outline, then, *Cymbeline* displays generic absorption and a reliance on the reversibility of time, both of which attributes are designed in the romances to overcome the absolute close of death. But it is precisely the matter of death that establishes Shakespeare's parodic use of the gestures of romance. For death in this play is less a threat or experience to be overcome than it is an occasion for mockery and excess.[10] Such mockery may be seen in the way that Shakespeare employs the hyperbolic presence of death, using such exaggeration to parody the conventional distinction between appearance and reality, as well as the distinction between the experience of mortality and the expectation of divinity. In fact, a case could be made that the characters never move beyond appearance and mortality, for there is no central consciousness or awareness that eventually illumines or resolves the play.

We have seen how the play establishes a series of refrains which, in intimating the need for rescue from death or the threat of death, set up the characteristic romance expectation of resolution by divinity. The experience or threat of death and violence is conspicuous throughout the play. The Queen, who wishes to kill Imogen, Pisanio, and Cymbeline, herself dies at the end of the play; Cloten wants to kill Posthumus and rape Imogen; Posthumus wants Pisanio to kill Imogen; Cloten is dead; Imogen is thought to be dead; Cymbeline believes his sons may be dead; the war between Britain and Rome promises death; Posthumus wants to be executed; Cymbeline wants to kill Iachimo, and unknowingly condemns his own son, disguised as Guiderius, for the death of Cloten.

So the plot of the play, to the point of excess, is garbed in death. Now if we examine the diverse threats of death, they all focus on one element: the characters' frail and finally humorous entrapment in mortality. Pressed to sum up this surfeit of death, one could hardly arrive at a better summary than Puck's line, "Lord, what fools these mortals be!" Death, in other words, is the principal context within which Shakespeare parodies the romances' customary movement beyond tragedy.[11]

Since a number of critics have argued that Posthumus and Imogen make up the central dramatic situation of the play, I feel obliged to demonstrate the presence of parody in what is often regarded as a serious, indeed tragic, action. Before doing so, however, let me say a few things about the center of the play. As I said earlier, I think the play is structurally a romance that experientially does not feel like one. This disjunction between structure or expectation and experience is informed by a parodic intention. Thematically, the parody is revealed through the mortality and, in some cases, the sheer stupidity of the characters. The characters are not rendered realistically so much as they are used as figures or embodiments of the disjunction between expectation and experience. Unlike the characters in *Pericles,* who move from analogy to identity, the characters in *Cymbeline* remain steadfastly locked into an analogical awareness, trapped, that is, in a set of expectations which are never quite fulfilled. This disjunction is evident not only within the characters and in the play's overt statement of theme; in addition, if one looks at the placement of characters within the play's twenty-seven scenes, it is clear that the characters hardly constitute the center of the play. Only one character appears in more than ten scenes, and that is Imogen. Of the remaining important characters, Cymbeline appears in six scenes, Posthumus in eight, Pisanio in eight, Iachimo in six, the Queen in five, Cloten in seven, Belarius, Arviragus, and Guiderius in five. This dispersal of characters—and dispersal is a characteristic feature of the play—has not been previously noted, or else it has not been thought important. But it is important because it shows the characters, or Shakespeare's concept of character in the play, as subsidiary to a much larger authorial intention—that of parody.

It is true that up until V.v Imogen, especially, is the central character in the sense that she travels through the play's three plots. No doubt this is why Marsh argues that Imogen "is the key figure. Her presence joins together the diverse parts of the story, and her unshakable virtue provides the standard by which all other actions are measured."[12] But Imogen is central primarily in a negative way, which is to say her centrality is largely the occasion for, and the focus of, parody. In Shakespeare's romances women customarily are either associated or invested with divine powers, and they are keys to the emergence of romance reunification. One immediately recalls Thaisa, Marina, Hermione, Paulina, Perdita, Miranda (to an extent), and Katherine in *Henry VIII*. Quite understandably, the tendency among critics has been to view Imogen in this light—after all, she is associated with faith and eternity. Just as the play sets up a pattern of refrains intimating the need for Providence, everything seems to point to Imogen as the heroine of the play. She is referred to as "Thou divine Imogen" (II.i.57); she is "More goddess-like than wife-like" (III.ii.8); Belarius associates her with divinity, calling her "an angel! or if not, / An earthly paragon!" (III.vi.42); she is a "blessed thing" (IV.ii.206); and Posthumus figurally thinks of her as "The temple / Of virtue" (V.v.220-21), much as Pericles sees Marina as a figure of Patience. But if these are the expectations she is designed to embody and promote, one might well ask, what purpose do they serve, and what happens to Imogen, as an alleged figure of divinity? The answer is that she is an "earthly paragon," to be sure, which translates in this case as the object of parody.

In I.vi, for example, we see that Imogen's principal defect is her susceptibility to seemingly divine appeals. Like Posthumus, she overestimates the divinity of being human, and underestimates her own, as well as Posthumus's, mortality. The whole wager, in fact, becomes the occasion for Shakespeare's parody of lofty expectations. Imogen successfully resists Iachimo's first appeal which is based on human mortality, but as soon as he says of Posthumus,

He sits 'mongst men like a [descended] god;
He hath a kind of honor sets him off,
More than a mortal seeming (I.vi.169-71)

Imogen responds, "All's well, sir. Take my pow'r i' th' court for yours" (I.vi.179). And Shakespeare proceeds to engage in some grisly sexual puns, clearly at the expense of Imogen's "honor," when she accepts Iachimo's trunk for safekeeping. She will protect his valuables, even as he will later itemize "The treasure of her honor" (II.ii.42). She says more than she knows when she promises that she will "pawn mine honor for their safety," and that the trunk "shall safe be kept, / And truly yielded you" (I.vi,194, 209-10).

Similarly, in II.iii Imogen's honor again becomes the target of assault and the occasion for parody. In light of many critics' fascination with Imogen's supposed divinity, this scene has been construed in a rather one-sided manner. The standard reading maintains that Cloten, as the monumentally inept suitor and ineffective villain, is the comic scapegoat of the scene, which he most certainly is. But Imogen is also a scapegoat. The scene opens with Cloten's obsession with "penetration" (II.iii.14, 27), and one can hardly forget the obscenity—Shakespeare's obscenity—in such lines as, "If you can penetrate her with our fingering, so; we'll try with tongue too" (II.iii.14-15). But if Cloten is an ass, we should remember that the occasion and subject of these lines is Imogen's honor. Moreover, even as Imogen later repudiates Cloten, telling him that Posthumus's "mean'st garment / That ever hath but clipt his body, is dearer / In my respect than all the hairs above thee" (II.iii.133-35), it turns out that in Act IV this rejection cuts two ways.

The standard reading of IV.i, Cloten's soliloquy, is that the joke is on Cloten. He appears dressed in Posthumus's garments, hoping that appearance will become reality, and declares "How fit his garments serve me. . . . it is not vainglory for a man and his glass to confer in his own chamber—I mean, the lines of my body are as well drawn as his; no less young, more strong. . . . Posthumus, thy head, which now is growing upon thy shoulders, shall within this hour be off" (IV.i.2-3, 7-10, 15-17).

Cloten is both right and wrong, both the subject of parody and its vehicle. He is not the heroic figure he thinks himself to be, and is therefore killed by Guiderius. But he is, evidently, substantially correct in his estimate of the lines of his body, for though it is his, not Posthumus's head, which is cut off, Imogen *does not* perceive any significant difference between his body and Posthumus's. When Imogen subsequently weeps over the headless body of Cloten, mistaking it for Posthumus, and exclaims "Oh, my lord, my lord?" (IV.ii.332), one is tempted to reply, my lord, indeed! One would think that Imogen, who was so certain of the difference between Cloten and her more than mortal Posthumus, could surely identify the body of her husband. But apparently her perception is as superficial as Cloten's, and this is precisely the point of Shakespeare's grotesque parody.[13] Like Cloten, she is unable to see through the "meanest garment," and neither can Posthumus, as we will see in Scene v of Act V.

Imogen's experience, however, is just one of a number of examples of parody in the play. In a sense, one might say that though the play lacks a thematic center, it certainly does not lack in skill or intelligent design. The dispersal of characters, for instance, activates the frequent disjunctions in the play, but the authorial intent of parody organizes the pattern of dispersal. Ordinarily the function of dispersal in the romances is to create a series of oppositions which are a paradigm of mortal and fallible perception, and these oppositions are either dissolved or transcended with the emergence of providential powers. To the extent that the characters are mortal, they move along, one might say, a horizontal line of awareness, perceiving their relationship to themselves, as well as to providence, in analogical terms. With the entrance of providence, in the form of a vision, dream, or oracle, the characters' level of awareness is directed vertically, rather than horizontally, and prior analogies, as in *Pericles,* become vehicles of identity—a kind of archetypal awareness grounded in theophany. In *Cymbeline* Shakespeare certainly promotes this expectation, as we have seen both in the refrain lines and in the association of Imogen with eternity, but characteristically this expectation functions as the basis for parody. The basis of parody may be demonstrated if we look at how Shakespeare presents the major perceptual problem of the play, and then in V.v refuses to solve it with a romance resolution. *Cymbeline* does move beyond tragedy, but refuses to attach that movement to the workings of eternal time.

Like the presence of death, the perceptual problem of *Cymbeline* is stated to the point of excess. The theme of reality and appearance—cliché that it is—is run into the ground. Characters continually report what they think, or wish others to think, that they have seen, and their reports are either unintentionally mistaken or deliberately false. The First Gentleman says of Posthumus, "I do not think / So fair an outward and such stuff within / Endows a man but he" (I.i.22-24), and the Second Gentleman characteristically states, "I honor him / Even out of your report" (I.i.54-55). Imogen later attacks Iachimo for slandering Posthumus, telling him "Thou wrong'st a gentleman, who is as far / From thy report as thou from honor" (I.v,145-46), and then in the next breath she falls for Iachimo's alternate plan, just as Posthumus later believes Iachimo's false report. Cloten, too, wants Imogen's lady to "Sell me your good report" (II.iii.83), and he falls victim to appearances. Once united with Belarius and her brothers in Wales, Imogen declares,

> These are kind creatures. Gods, what lies I have heard!
> Our courtiers say all's savage but at court.
> Experience, O, thou disprov'st report! (IV.ii.32-34)

She is, typically, both right and wrong. She is among friends, but there is savagery in Wales (the death of Cloten and war); and she is soon to mistake Cloten's body for Posthumus's which suggests the limitations of her acquisition of experience.

Perhaps Posthumus best summarizes how the acquisition of experience is designed to overcome perceptual discrepancies and yet eventually fails to do so. Now remorseful, though characteristically mistaken about the death of Imogen, Posthumus chooses to disguise himself as a "Briton peasant" to defend his country. He desires to

> Let me make men know
> More valor in me than my habits show.
> Gods, put the strength o' th' Leonati in me!
> To shame the guise o' th' world, I will begin
> The fashion; less without and more within. (V.i.29-33)

Later he does display his valor as a Briton peasant, but his action hardly shames "the guise o' th' world," if we take the phrase to refer to mistaken perceptions and expectations. His desire for, and expectation of, death is never satisfied, and his inability to see through "without" to "within" is evident in the later scene when he cannot recognize his own wife, though Pisanio can! If anything, Posthumus, like Imogen and Cymbeline, does not so much shame "the guise o' th' world" as represent it.

Customarily all these perceptual discrepancies would be resolved at the end of the play. Interestingly, but no doubt consistently, the conclusion of the play conveys the *appearance* of resolution, but that resolution is so fragmented and dispersed as to suggest not the presence, but the parody, of romance. The theophany in V.iv, for example, is totally unlike that in any of the other romances, though it is entirely consistent with a parodic intent. When Jupiter, whom Felperin has aptly called "a divine lame-duck,"[14] appears to Posthumus—and in the productions I have seen this is invariably a funny moment—he does not solve anything. To the contrary: he complicates the play still further, and gives the appearance of being a kind of crotchety trickster. He tells Posthumus:

> Be not with mortal accidents oppres'd.
> No care of yours it is, you know 'tis ours.
> Whom best I love, I cross; to make my gift,
> The more delay'd, delighted. (V.iv.99-102)

Jupiter here sounds rather like Prospero, who will tell Miranda:

> Be collected.
> No more amazement. Tell your piteous heart
> There's no harm done. (I.ii.13-15)

> but this swift business
> I must uneasy make, lest too light winning
> Make the prize light. (I.ii.451-53)

But the difference between Prospero and Jupiter is the difference between the intent to resolve and the intent to complicate—the difference, in short, between romance and parody.

Jupiter, in effect, tells Posthumus that what is happening to him is none of his business. And to prove this, he presents Posthumus with a riddle, which Posthumus hopes is "not, as is our fangled world, a garment / Nobler than it covers!" (V.iv.134-35). The riddle brings us back to garments, the source of so much confusion in the play, and back to the disjunction between appearance and reality. Even if we concede that the riddle is eventually solved by the Soothsayer who has had prior difficulties with his own prophecy, it still turns out that the riddle does not resolve the play. Moreover, the riddle and the appearance of Jupiter are gratuitous because they affect only Posthumus, and he is in no position to resolve the play. What dominates V.v is not providential harmony but the dispersed awareness of the "fangled world," as we can see in the following outline of the successive stages of the play's ostensible resolution:

1. The Queen is dead.
2. Cornelius reports her confession that she hated and intended to kill Imogen and Cymbeline, and that she intended to make Cloten king.
3. Lucius asks that Fidele be spared.
4. Fidele sees Iachimo's ring.
5. Belarius recognizes Fidele, whom he thought dead.
6. Pisanio recognizes Fidele to be Imogen.
7. Fidele questions Iachimo.
8. Posthumus wonders why.
9. Iachimo confesses.
10. Posthumus reveals himself.
11. Posthumus slaps Imogen who is about to reveal her identity.
12. Pisanio identifies Imogen.

13. Cornelius explains Imogen's apparent death.
14. Belarius now understands his mistaken view of Fidele's death.
15. Pisanio talks about Cloten.
16. Guiderius confesses that he killed Cloten.
17. Cymbeline condemns him to death.
18. Belarius reveals Cymbeline's two sons.
19. Cymbeline forgives Belarius (Morgan) and wants to go to the temple.
20. Posthumus forgives Iachimo.
21. Posthumus asks for an interpretation of his dreams and the riddle.
22. The Soothsayer interprets the dream and riddle.
23. Cymbeline offers to pay the tribute to the Romans.
24. The characters leave for the temple of Jupiter.

Every reader of the play has been struck, not to say astonished, by this conclusion. The conclusion is totally unlike that of any of the romances, not to mention Shakespeare's other plays. The successive revelations, if such they be, are not so much continuous as contiguous, lined up side by side rather than melding into a whole. This dispersal of partial insight, which is an analogue to the play's disjunctive structure, amounts in my view to a collective parody—a sort of put-on of what romance is supposed to do, but in this case does not accomplish. Instead of being struck by a sense of wonder, one is aware more of the manner of accomplishment than of its effect. Experience is continually set against expectation; the characters strive to experience a sense of eternity but remain trapped at the level of mortality. Every revelation is partial, to the point of distraction, and consecutive rather than cumulative. Some critics, like Rabkin, may choose to regard this scene as Shakespeare's display of his own art, but I believe a more compelling view, one more closely related to the audience's experience of this scene, is that Shakespeare here uses his own art to parody not only the conventions of a romance resolution, but the way in which all the characters are enclosed within the artifice of their own mortal limitations.

The ostensible thematic intent of this philharmonic resolution is stated repeatedly, possibly insistently. Posthumus tells Iachimo, "Live, / And deal with others better" (V.v.419-20); Cymbeline asserts that "Pardon's the word to all" (422) and that the fault lies primarily with "our wicked queen, / Whom heavens, in justice both on her and hers, / Have laid most heavy hand" (463-65). And the Soothsayer seemingly tidies up all the play's loose ends by declaring the official aims of Shakespearean romance: "The fingers of the pow'rs above do tune / The harmony of this peace" (466-67).

There is just one problem with all this apparent ecstasy, and that problem has been precisely described by Joan Hartwig: "Serious matters are constantly undergoing dislocation by comic perspectives which the characters cannot seem to refrain from creating by their human gestures. These gestures keep the resolution from being patent and suggest that the lesson the characters have learned may not be as fully effective as a formulaic resolution would provide."[15] In short, there exists a considerable difference between what the characters claim has happened, and what in fact has occurred. They claim harmony in the midst of comic dispersal; they claim a comprehensive awareness which is nowhere apparent; they claim the presence of divinity, even though the Soothsayer, who acts as the official interpreter of providence, has already been wrong once, though he has displayed a remarkable talent for prophecy in retrospect.

At one point, in response to the Soothsayer's interpretation, Cymbeline declares, "This hath some seeming" (V.v.452). In saying this, Cymbeline at once speaks for what the characters want the play to be, and alludes to the disjunction between the characters' expectations and the audience's awareness. Unlike the characters who go through the motions of experiencing romance, the audience is less enthralled by the alleged presence of heavenly harmony than it is entertained by the "fingers" of Shakespearean parody. It is no wonder, therefore, that this play's ostensible resolution does not occur, as in the other romances, on sacred ground, for the characters have not arrived at their expected destination.

FIVE

The Issues of
The Winter's Tale

If *Pericles* and *Cymbeline* explicitly display the conventions of romance—the former as a pure exercise in romance, the latter as a parody of that purity—*The Winter's Tale* takes those conventions and invests them with extraordinary human significance. One way *The Winter's Tale* generates its power is through the continual employment of both latent and explicit versions of contention. Not only do the characters frequently contend with one another, but whole sections of the play stand in opposition to one another, though the opposition is less a rigid contrast than an unfolding process, drawing on different generic perspectives, which culminates in the romance absorption of diverse experiences in V.iii.

Furthermore, there may be a latent level of contention in the play between the audience's experience of the play and the dramatic expectations that Shakespeare initially builds up but subsequently undermines. This level of contention, which is most visible in the statue scene of V.iii, seems designed to achieve a simultaneous experience of romance shared at the same moment by the audience and the characters. As John Taylor observes, "What the play 'seems to say' is a counsel of the most ecstatic patience, and I believe patience is the word for the peculiar state in which we witness the latter part of it—how often can we practice the virtue celebrated by a work of art in its presence?"[1] But there is evidence much earlier in the play that Shakespeare is, among other things, attempting to dislocate the audience's dramatic expectations, particularly as they relate to a norm of reality that distinguishes between the absolute close of tragedy and the experience of romance. At the very least, as William Matchett has argued, "Shakespeare's problem in *The Winter's Tale* is that of compressing a complete tragedy into the first half in order to pass through and beyond it in the second."[2]

One feature of the play's language may establish an illuminating entrance into the play's use of romance conventions, as well as its enactment of the experience of romance. At key points the source of contention in the play seems to be the characters' diverse understandings and uses of the word *issue*. On a purely statistical basis, no other Shakespearean play approximates the relative frequency the word has in *The Winter's Tale*.[3] But since we all know that even if statistics do not lie, liars may use statistics, it is essential to establish the word's importance beyond simply stating its statistical presence as a self-evident fact. Of the meanings of "issue" recorded in the *OED*, the following play a significant role in *The Winter's Tale*: (1) the power of going, passing or flowing out; egress, exit; (2) outgoing; termination, end; close; (3) a place or means of egress; way out; outlet; (4) offspring, progeny; a child or children; a descendant or descendants; (5) outcome of an action (the event or fortune befalling a person); (6) (Medicine) a discharge of blood or other matter from the body due to disease; (7) (Law) the point or question, at the conclusion of the pleadings between contending parties in an action, when one side affirms and the other denies.

Naturally, to say that these diverse meanings operate in the play is to run the risk of turning a dramatic experience into a semantic exercise, rather like the Soothsayer's philological explications in *Cymbeline*. But if I can show that these meanings expand the conventions and contribute to the experience of romance, then, though I may lack the Soothsayer's prophetic intention, I shall at least enjoy the advantage of critical hindsight. I should also say that my initial examination of *issue* will presume a context which I shall develop later: namely, that the play does generally divide into three parts (I-III.ii, III.iii-IV, V) as others have suggested,[4] but I will go further and argue that these three parts represent, respectively, the conventions and experience of tragedy, pastoral comedy, and romance. It is not until Act V, which is at once the end of tragedy and the beginning of romance, that the principal attributes of romance surface explicitly.

Moreover, though the first three acts represent what is "lost" in the play, it is not exactly true to say that Acts IV and V dramatize what is "found," taking Perdita to be the "lost one." For Perdita is found (by report) in V.ii; thus what provides V.iii, the statue scene, with its unique experience of romance is that in this scene *more* than what was lost is found. The discovery of Hermione is, to quote Matchett, "not something we knew all the time; it is not even a miracle which is reported to us or staged for us; it is a miracle in the full effect of which we participate."[5]

Few if any will argue that the first three acts of *The Winter's Tale* are something other than tragic, though on strictly realistic grounds the basis of the tragedy appears rather implausible. The movement from the serenity of I.i to Leontes's sudden rage early in I.ii is, to say the least, disruptive, and this movement is only the first of a number of instances in the play that dislocate the audience's expectations. The initial source of contention, which is hinted at in I.i and dramatized in I.ii, has to do with sons specifically and with childhood or the distant past generally. The matter of time and timing, as it relates to crucial human events, is established early in the play and continued throughout. In I.ii, for example, we are told that Polixenes has been in Sicilia nine months (I.ii.1), that Leontes had to wait "Three crabbed months" (102) before Hermione accepted his marriage proposal, and Leontes says, "Looking on the lines / Of my boy's face, methoughts I did recoil / Twenty-three years, and saw myself unbreech'd / In my green velvet coat" (153-56). I mention these uses of time to estabish a context for the first use of *issue* which explicitly refers to sons, but which carries with it a sense of time relating both to the present (Mamillius as son and Hermione as pregnant wife), and recoiling to the distant past (Leontes as son, suitor, and father). Thus, in his initial rage which is played against a backdrop of an awareness of time, Leontes attacks Hermione through Mamillius:

> Go play, boy, play. Thy mother plays, and I
> Play too, but so disgrac'd a part, whose issue
> Will hiss me to my grave. (187-89)

There are at least two uses of issue in this speech; the one, reinforced by the theatrical metaphor, suggests that the outcome of
Leontes's part (a cuckold) will hiss him to his grave, while the other
use alludes to the imminent birth of Hermione's child which will
supposedly confirm his cuckoldry. Throughout the first three acts
Leontes's fixation is always on the latter use of issue (namely, a bastard child), as we can see in the two other instances when he uses
the term: "This brat is none of mine, / It is the issue of Polixenes"
(II.iii.93-94); and "No! I'll not rear / Another's issue" (II.iii.192-
93). Now all of this is fairly obvious, and contributes toward the es-
tablishment of the explicit tragedy of the first three acts. What may
not be so obvious is that Leontes's accusation in the present implies
a massive disruption of the past. Or, to put it another way, every
contention in the present implies a latent contention with the past.
Moreover, so long as characters are dislocated from the past they
will remain in a tragic condition.

The use of issue, meaning sons, thus raises all sorts of additional
questions relating to diverse aspects of time—the past (boyhood),
the present (adulthood and marriage), the future (heirs and descendants). For example, we have seen how, looking on his son,
Leontes thinks back twenty-three years; similarly, when Leontes
tells Hermione, "thou never spok'st / To better purpose" (I.ii.88-
89), Hermione leads him back to the time of their betrothal. But
Shakespeare reaches even further back; commenting on the time
when he and Leontes were boys, Polixenes says to Hermione:

> We were, fair Queen,
> Two lads that thought there was no more behind
> But such a day to-morrow as to-day,
> And to be boy eternal. (I.ii.62-65)

Sons, and boyhood generally, thus function as aspects of both past
and present time; every present appearance of sons, as an "issue,"

carries with it an analogue to the past. The above quotation, for instance, alludes to the regenerative role of childhood, and it will subsequently contribute to romance's reversibility of time. Sons are associated with comfort, and they also perform a medicinal function—they discharge diseases, another version of issue. Camillo says of Mamillius: "It is a gallant child; one that, indeed, physics the subject, makes old hearts fresh" (I.i.38 39); and Polixenes later comments about Florizel: "He makes a July's day short as December, / And with his varying childness cures in me / Thoughts that would thick my blood" (I.ii.169-71). Indeed, this is why in V.i Leontes's old heart can only begin to become fresh when his lost son is regained through the acquisition of a new son-in-law, Florizel, who is welcomed by Leontes "As is the spring to th' earth!" (V.i.152). Florizel replaces Mamillius, just as the birth of romance replaces the death of tragedy, and this may be why Shakespeare, characteristically withholding evidence until the last moment, has Paulina abruptly announce:

> Had our prince [Mamillius],
> Jewel of children, seen this hour, he had pair'd
> Well with this lord [Florizel]; there was not full a month
> Between their births. (V.i.115-18)

As the initial "issue" of the play, sons simultaneously contribute to the play's tragic backdrop and its romance resolution. They are tragic to the extent that they are either lost or dead, or associated with bastardy and adultery, as in Leontes's diseased imagination. They are tragic because their apparent actions disrupt the flow of time and life. On the other hand, sons are necessary to the resolution of tragedy to the degree that they perform medicinal or purgative functions, as Florizel does for Leontes, restore the flow of social and familial order, and re-introduce the natural process of "great creating Nature" which is the fulfilled cycle of birth, maturity, and decline.

Of course, the "issue" of chidren in the play does not refer just to sons. Hermione gives birth to a daughter, Perdita, who continues the long line of innocent daughters—Marina, Imogen, later Miranda, and the baby Elizabeth—who are necessary to the resolution of romance. Although Leontes treats the baby as a bastard issue, Paulina clearly sees the baby and her presentation of it as a potential purgation of Leontes's diseased imagination. Holding the baby, Pauline tells Leontes:

> I
> Do come with words as medicinal as true,
> Honest as either, to purge him of that humor
> That presses him from sleep. (II.iii.36-39)

These medicinal words all refer to what Leontes calls a "female bastard," but it becomes increasingly apparent that Paulina, on her own authority, is not capable of resolving the numerous contentions within the play.[6] Here we arrive at another convention of romance that we have seen in the two earlier plays: namely, that individuals alone may precipitate or initiate a tragedy but they cannot solve it. Conversely, children, as we have seen, contain within themselves the potential for resolution—symbolically at least—but they are not capable, on their own, of restoring life.

By the time the oracle of Apollo is announced (III.ii.132-36), the cause of the tragedy is publicly stated and denounced, but its solution is at best problemmatical. Any number of characters, some of them quite minor, have consistently doubted Leontes's sense of the play's basic "issue," as we can see in the diverse observations of Camillo, Antigonus, and a Lord. Camillo refuses to murder Polixenes because

> if ever fearful
> To do a thing, where I the issue doubted,
> .   .   .   .
> 'twas a fear
> Which oft infects the wisest. (I.ii.258-59, 61-62)

Antigonus believes that Leontes is "abused" by "some putter-on" and assures Leontes that if his charges against Hermione prove true, then he "had rather glib myself than they [his daughters] / Should not produce fair issue" (II.i.149-50). And a Lord, certain that Leontes is wrong, implores him "that you do change this purpose, / Which being so horrible, so bloody, must / Lead on to some foul issue" (II.iii.151-53).

But if characters, on their own, are able to determine what is right or wrong, can they also authoritatively demonstrate their conclusions and correct these wrongs? Only one character appears to have this kind of authority—Paulina—but I would argue that her authority stems from a divine sanction which raises an additional version of *issue* in the first three acts. Emilia says to Paulina:

> Your honor and your goodness is so evident
> That your free undertaking cannot miss
> A thriving issue. There is no lady living
> So meet for this great errand. (II.ii.41-44)

By "thriving issue," I take Emilia-to be referring both to the birth of Perdita and to the, presumably, successful reversal of Leontes's jealousy as a result of that birth. But that same birth has the immediate effect of precipitating—at least ostensibly—the three tragic deaths of Mamillius, Hermione, and Perdita, events which Paulina in the first three acts is unable to resolve. On the other hand, though, Paulina is associated with the "thriving issue" that eventually dominates Acts IV and V—namely romance—and she becomes the spokesman in Sicilia, as Camillo is in Bohemia, for the play's pendulum swing away from tragedy toward the beginning of romance.

The final and most important meaning of *issue* which develops in Act III is the legal one. Leontes chooses to put Hermione on public trial in Act III, and his accusations against her are put to a divine trial at the oracle of Apollo. This sense of trial is further elaborated when Dion, returning from the oracle, proclaims:

> (Thus by Apollo's great divine seal'd up)
> Shall the contents discover, something rare

Even then will rush to knowledge. Go; fresh horses!
And gracious be the issue! (III.i.19-22)

Dion is referring to the outcome of Apollo's verdict, but that outcome, as drama, is paradoxical. Hermione is innocent, but the conclusion of III.ii is anything but innocent, for three people are be-
lieved dead. For all intents and purposes, therefore, by the end of
III.ii all possible avenues of individual initiative have been exhausted, save for the cryptic verdict from Apollo which, in the eyes
of the characters, may appear superfluous. There is no evident way,
from the vantage point of either characters or audience, that a solution will emerge which will answer to the oracle's condition that
"the King shall live without an heir, if that which is lost be not
found" (III.ii.134-36). The play's tragic action has spent itself, but
the play also appears to be at a standstill.

This sense of a standstill, which reflects the characters' and perhaps the audience's limited abilities to see a way out, devolves from
the compressed, short-run view of time that is associated with
tragic irreversibility. What happens in the remainder of the play is
that the major issue is no longer just filial, medicinal, or legal: it is
dramatic and experiential, in the sense that the final trial, for both
the characters and the audience, settles down to a contest between
the forces and conventions of tragedy (e.g., Acts I–III.ii) and the
evolution and development of romance in Acts III.iii–V. These
forces are alluded to at the end of Act III, which I see as a turn away
from the remainder of the preceding acts, and implemented in Acts
IV and V. If tragedy deals with what is lost, then romance deals
with what is found. This pendulum movement from tragedy to romance is clearly evident in III.iii which, though it dramatizes the simultaneity of birth and death, finally settles on birth and the life
forces associated with romance. Antigonus dies, though it is a "natural" death unlike the others of Act III, for a bear, not a man, kills
him; similarly, the sailors are drowned by a storm. But before Antigonus dies, he has a remarkable vision of a dead Hermione in
which he both leads and misleads the audience. He says

> I do believe
> Hermione hath suffer'd death, and that
> Apollo would (this being indeed the issue
> Of King Polixenes) it should here be laid
> Either for life or death, upon the earth
> Of its right father. Blossom, speed thee well! (III.iii.41-46)

This speech suggests several things about the remainder of the play and its basic "issue." The audience knows that Perdita is not the issue of Polixenes because the oracle has declared Hermione chaste. But like Antigonus, the audience has every reason to believe that Hermione is dead. Still, if these two matters are reasonably certain, the larger issue—the trial between the forces of tragedy and whatever happens beyond tragedy—remains in doubt. Among other things, the audience might at this point reasonably ask itself: how is Shakespeare going to get out of this one? One way that Shakespeare begins to settle this issue is by using Perdita as both the consummation of tragedy and the commencement of romance; she is laid, that is, "Either for life, or death, upon the earth," and, moreover, the earlier tragic issue of paternity is now transferred away from the human to the natural (the earth) which is the "right father," just as Perdita becomes less important as a person than as a "Blossom," who speaks the pastoral language of flowers in Act IV. Shakespeare has used this short scene as the exhaustion of tragedy (in death) and the provisional entrance of pastoral comedy (in the natural reemergence of life associated with spring). The audience, like the shepherd, has been moved to the point where we, too, might exclaim: "Now bless thyself; thou met'st with things dying. I with things new born" (III.iii.112-13).[7] And what we are led to witness in Acts IV and V is the birth and consummation of Shakespearean romance.

The movement from death to birth and rebirth surfaces explicitly beginning with IV.ii, but the intellectual basis for this change of direction is described in IV.i, a scene with no evident parallel in Shakespeare's other romances. This scene provides us with the closest approximation to Shakespeare's explanation of the basis of romance. There are, of course, many passages in a number of Shakespeare's plays where time is a subject, but there is no other scene where Time speaks for itself—and for Shakespeare as well. I have repeatedly argued in this book that one of the key conceptions of Shakespearean romance is the reversibility of time, the turn away from tragedy's absolute close. This turn away begins in III.iii, with the pendulum swing from death to life, but the rationale for the distinctive turn toward romance is explained—indeed, argued for, as opposed to dramatized—in IV.i. It is unusual enough just to have a character named Time, but the presence of that character signals the play's rise to an emblematic awareness or consciousness through which the audience will have to revise its own reality principle. Twice in Act III this emblematic awareness is alluded to; first when Hermione declares:

> But thus, if pow'rs divine
> Behold our human actions (as they do),
> I doubt not then but innocence shall make
> False accusation blush, and tyranny
> Tremble at Patience. (III.ii.29-32)

The second time is when Antigonus, in his vision of Hermione, describes her as appearing "in pure white robes, / Like very sanctity" (III.iii.22-23). With the entrance of Time in IV.i, however, Shakespeare raises the perceptual level of the play to a systematically emblematic awareness, thereby enacting a form of drama where "powers divine" do "Behold our human actions." Indeed in Acts IV and V it becomes increasingly apparent, as J. H. P. Pafford has suggested, that "*The Winter's Tale* is not the story of one person or even of a group of persons but rather of passions, virtues, and actions."[8]

Interestingly, Time addresses itself to the audience in such a way that it both is and presents several versions of *issue*. Time, that is, appears in the guise of a trial (one form of issue) of the audience's conventional expectations; it represents the issue of growth (through Perdita and Florizel); and it forecasts the issue or outcome of the play. In the first usage, Time claims to "try all, both joy and terror / Of good and bad" (IV.i.1-2), and far more assertively maintains, "it is in my pow'r / To o'erthrow law, and in one self-born hour / To plant, and o'erwhelm custom" (7-9). Here Time evidently speaks for Shakespeare's defiant use of romance, which is a mode of drama that does, indeed, overthrow the laws and customs of conventional drama. In this sense, then, Time presents a trial, just as the remainder of the play conducts a trial of the audience's expectations—of our ability, for example, to accept the proposition that one way of proceeding beyond tragedy is to skip over sixteen years and start all over again. Moreover, Time stands for a dimension of growth beyond death; it reenacts and revitalizes the prior issue of children. Although Time leaves "the growth untried / Of that wide gap [sixteen years]" (IV.i.6-7), it assures us that the play's subject will be "th' freshest things now reigning" (13), that Time will give his "scene such growing / As you had slept between" (16-17), and that a visible manifestation of how the issue of children in the first three acts has been transformed through the magic of Time is Perdita, the lost child of the past, who is "now grown in grace / Equal with wond'ring" (24-25). Finally, Time draws on the use of *issue* as outcome, both of a trial and a drama, when it says of Perdita: "What of her ensues / I list not prophesy; but let Time's news / Be known when 'tis brought forth" (25-27). In other words, through Perdita the audience will observe a process which Panofsky has described as follows: "Only by destroying spurious values can Time fulfill the office of unveiling Truth. Only as a principle of alteration can he reveal his truly universal power."[9]

I have enumerated, perhaps too scrupulously, the varying uses of *issue* not as an exercise in semantic juggling but to point to the varying levels of contention or trial in the play. For the moment, Time appears to place the audience in a vantage point superior to that of the characters who remain locked in the tragedy of Sicilia. We know that Perdita is alive; Leontes and the others do not. We, as the audience, are experientially beyond the tragedy of Acts I–III, but again Leontes and the court of Sicilia are not. Thus there is an experiential bifurcation not only dividing the first three acts from Act IV, but dividing the old characters of the first three acts from the new characters of Act IV. To put it another way, the audience that witnesses, and the characters who participate in, Act IV exist in a realm of "new" time—we are starting all over—whereas Leontes, who is absent in Act IV, continues to be trapped in a tragic past, performing a "saint-like sorrow" (V.i.2). These two versions of time preserve our sense of a tragic past based on Time as destroyer ("things dying" or being lost) as well as our present experience of the movement toward romance based on Time as revealer ("things new born" or being found). But though Act IV reverses and incorporates the time and events of Acts I–III and begins to proceed beyond tragedy, it does not follow that Act IV is itself a romance. For one thing, the court of Sicilia is absent from Act IV, and this is why the two remaining properties of Shakespearean romance—its absorptive capacity and the presence of hierophany—are missing until Act V. Act IV, I believe, is a pastoral comedy which, set against the preceding acts, preserves the bifurcation of tragicomedy. This bifurcation is expressed through the conventional pastoral contrast between rural simplicity and court complexity. Moreover, in regathering and recycling a prior tragedy, the pastoral comedy of Act IV performs what Hallett Smith has called "the central meaning of pastoral . . . the rejection of the aspiring mind,"[10] thereby preparing the way for the advent of romance in Act V.

One way of demonstrating how Act IV recycles the prior tragedy of Acts I–III.ii is through examining its recapitulative procedures, which have been noted by other critics.[11] For every crucial tragic event in the first three acts there occurs a comic analogue in Act IV, and this process of matching and transforming preserves the tragicomic bifurcation which will not be absorbed and resolved until Act V. As I shall try to show, however, the analogues of Act IV, although they duplicate or perhaps replicate key events of the tragic past, are placed within the general context of the conventions of pastoral comedy. Perdita, for example, says, "Methinks I play as I have seen them do / In Whitsun pastorals" (IV.iv.133-34), but the key to our awareness of the pastoral comedy is a character who has no analogue in the prior acts—Autolycus.[12]

Very early in IV.ii Polixenes starts the issue of children over again when he asks Camillo: "Say to me, when saw'st thou the Prince Florizel, my son? Kings are no less unhappy, their issue not being gracious, than they are in losing them when they have approv'd their virtues" (IV.ii.25-28). Structurally, what occurs in the remainder of Act IV is that Florizel and Perdita play out youthful, innocent versions of the courtship of Leontes and Hermione, while Polixenes occupies the role of jealous father which is analogous to Leontes's earlier role as jealous husband. This is another version of the sort of "recoil" where a character contains both past and present meaning, both a destructive and potentially regenerative import. Later in Act IV Camillo has a vision of what will occur when Florizel and Perdita go to Leontes in Sicilia:

> Methinks I see
> Leontes opening his free arms and weeping
> His welcome forth; asks thee there, son, forgiveness,
> As 'twere i' th' father's person; kisses the hands
> Of your fresh princess; o'er and o'er divides him
> 'Twixt his unkindness and his kindness: th' one
> He chides to hell, and bids the other grow
> Faster than thought or time. (IV.iv.547-54)

This division between unkindness and kindness, chiding to hell and bidding to grow, points to both the duplication and the differences of Acts I–III and Act IV.

In both sections of the play a jealous older male, either as father or as husband, disrupts a marriage or impending marriage and precipitates what has the appearance of tragedy. When Paulina tries to talk to Leontes about Hermione's innocence and about the baby Perdita, Leontes asks: "[What] noise there, ho?" (II.iii.39), to which Paulina responds, "No noise, my lord, but needful conference" (40). A quite similar confrontation occurs when Florizel tells the disguised Polixenes to observe his betrothal to Perdita, "Mark our contract" (IV.iv.417), which prompts Polixenes to reveal himself and exclaim, "Mark your divorce, young sir, / Whom son I dare not call" (417-18). Polixenes, like Leontes, immediately alludes to the "issue" of children as bastards, and of course he regards Perdita as being lowborn. Similarly, just as Polixenes flees Sicilia with the assistance and counsel of Camillo at the end of I.ii, so at the end of IV.iv Florizel and Perdita flee Bohemia under the guidance of Camillo. Moreover, Camillo, like Paulina whom he will marry at the end of the play, performs a medicinal function (another version of *issue*) for Florizel and Perdita; Florizel addresses Camillo as "Preserver of my father, now of me, / The medicine of our house" (IV.iv.586-87).

Despite these parallels, however, three basic attributes of Act IV differentiate its comic impulse from the tragic experience of the preceding acts. First, the whole of the fourth act occurs in a regenerative pastoral context—flowers, sheep-shearing, chastity, songs, mystical rites—whereas the prior tragedy occurs at court. Secondly, in contrast to Leontes's abandonment of Hermione, Florizel is absolutely unwavering in his love of Perdita, so much so that he tells the fearful girl: "Lift up thy looks. / From my succession wipe me, father, I / Am heir to my affection" (IV.iv.479-81). If Leontes is madly out of love, Florizel, whose senses are "better pleas'd with madness" (484), is madly in love. But the third and most distinctive property of the pastoral comedy in Act IV arises from the presence of Autolycus, who celebrates the sheer vitality of life, and who gives distinctive voice to the pastoral ethos of Act IV.

The whole of Act IV is dotted with Autolycus's songs and capers, and it is fascinating to watch how these songs symbolically or emblematically allude to the past of tragedy at the same time that they exude the spirit of pastoral comedy. Autolycus's first song, which opens IV.iii, sets the tone for the remainder of the act. In this song he declares that "the red blood reigns in the winter's pale," that "a quart of ale is a dish for a king," that his mode of lyric is "summer songs" (rather than winter's tales), and that though he is "out of service" (that is, removed from the court),

shall I go mourn for that, my dear?
The pale moon shines by night;
And when I wander here and there,
I then do most go right. (IV.iii.15-18)

Autolycus's song exudes a natural force that supersedes the tragic
self-assertiveness of the court. Like Perdita, his songs are a pastoral
blossom, albeit tainted, that signal the play's growth and contin-
uance of life.

In alluding to court life and loss ("the winter's pale" [tale?],
"dish for a king," "service," "mourn"), Autolycus preserves the
audience's sense of the past three acts; yet he also recycles that past
through his songs that assert time's ability to transform tragedy. Indeed, the song that concludes IV.iii alludes to the essential time differences between the compressed and destructive experience of tragedy and the reversal of tragic time that occurs in Act IV:

Jog on, jog on, the foot-path way,
And merrily hent the stile-a;
A merry heart goes all the day.
Your sad tires in a mile-a. (IV.iii.123-26)

Like Autolycus, Act IV jogs on merrily in the mode of pastoral
comedy, and it seems entirely appropriate that Florizel—the "issue"
of Act IV—should transform his own appearance by adopting the
disguise of Autolycus's clothes. Symbolically, this exchange of garments duplicates the fourth act's transformation of apparent tragedy, with Florizel adopting the pastoral guise of Autolycus and thus
rejecting court aspirations, though Autolycus, comically echoing
the tragic severity of the first three acts, believes that his exchange
of garments with Florizel is a sure sign that "this is the time that
the unjust man doth thrive" (IV.iv.673-74).

The principal effect of all these pastoral devices is to blunt, even
as it alludes to, the tragedy of the first three acts, and to transform
the basic issue of the play. Indeed, the leisurely length of Act IV
(approximately 1100 lines) reflects the pastoral transformation of

the tragic experience of Acts I–III. But scale is not the only alteration in the "issues." Rather, as I have tried to show, Shakespeare
sets up replacements for the preceding acts within the new context
of pastoral comedy. If one of the issues of Acts I–III is bastard children, the same issue appears in altered form in Act IV. If another issue of the first three acts is Leontes's diseased imagination, then Polixenes repeats that issue, but Camillo, as a medicinal preserver,
purges the infection. Similarly, where the trials, as another version
of issue, of Acts I–III.ii lead to apparent death, the trials of Act IV,
beginning with Time's challenge to the audience, create new life by
supplanting and incorporating past tragedies. No less important,
the dominant mode of discourse in Act IV, as we have already seen
in Autolycus's songs, is the pastoral language of organic growth
(another version of issue) projected through music, dance, the seasons, sexual vitality, and just plain fun and frolic. Many critics, of
course, have focused on the Art-Nature debate between Perdita and
Polixenes, but I would argue that the intellectual content and resolution of the debate is less important than the manner in which it
is conducted. Even though this debate continues to allude to the issue of bastards (IV.iv.83, 99), its language is consistently pastoral;
through its heavy references to flowers and the seasons the scene
linguistically duplicates the regenerative processes of nature, just as
the whole of Act IV, as pastoral comedy, recycles and regenerates
the prior tragedy of Acts I–III.

Generically, what distinguishes the tragedy of Acts I–III.ii from
Acts III.iii and IV is that the former is dominated by individual human actions in the court while the latter transforms those human
actions into processes associated with nature. The difference is between finite human perception and an emblematic awareness, between tragic self-assertiveness and pastoral submission, between a
compressed and an expanded understanding of time. But the resolution of the play does not strictly reside within nature, as in pastoral
comedy. Rather nature itself in Act V becomes an emblem of eternity, and this we can see in the absorptive capacity of Act V which
regathers the prior issues of the play as they have appeared within

the divergent contexts of tragedy and pastoral comedy, ultimately resolving them through the agency of romance.

Act V begins by repeatedly referring to the past issues of the first three acts. Dion cautions Paulina:

> consider little
> What dangers, by his Highness' fail of issue,
> May drop upon his kingdom, and devour
> Incertain lookers-on. (V.i.26-29)

But Paulina counsels Leontes to "Care not for issue, / The crown will find an heir" (46-47). The key sense of "issue," however, occurs when Leontes receives Florizel. In this remarkable speech Leontes draws together the various issues of the play at the very moment when he, paradoxically, regards himself as "issueless":

> The blessed gods
> Purge all infection from our air whilest you
> Do climate here! You have a holy father,
> A graceful gentleman, against whose person,
> (So sacred as it is) I have done sin,
> For which the heavens, taking angry note,
> Have left me issueless; and your father's bless'd
> (As he from heaven merits it) with you,
> Worthy his goodness. What might I have been,
> Might I a son and daughter now have look'd on,
> Such goodly things as you? (V.i.168-78)

I earlier observed that while Acts I–IV enact two of the principles of romance, a tragic backdrop and the use of reversible time to proceed beyond tragedy, the two other distinctive properties of romance, that is, the absorptive capacity of romance and its consummation in hierophany, remain to appear. Here in Leontes's speech all four characteristics begin to come together, even though the speaker believes himself to be issueless. Leontes continually refers

back to the tragic past of the prior acts, but the audience, which unlike Leontes has experienced the reversal of time in Act IV, knows
that the tragic past has been, to some extent, regenerated. We
know that Leontes is not issueless, for Perdita is alive. Similarly, the
lines "What might I have been, / Might I a son and daughter have
looked on, / Such goodly things as you" may be read, I believe, as
both a reference to the displacement of children in the past (one version of *issue*), and at the same time an allusion to the regenerative re-
placement of children in the present. That is, in one sense Leontes is
referring to Polixenes's good fortune (he is not issueless) of having
acquired a daughter (i.e., daughter-in-law), to add to his son, Florizel, though Polixenes does not at this time share Leontes's enthusiasm. But it is just as easy to construe the lines as Leontes's lament
that, on seeing Florizel and Perdita, he is reminded of his ostensibly
lost son and daughter (Mamillius and Perdita), whom he would like
to look on because they look like Florizel and Perdita. Such a reading is reinforced by Leontes's use of "Might I have been" and
"might." But, though he does not know it, that "might" has occurred; he is not entirely issueless though Mamillius remains lost.
The basic point, however, is that past and present have come together through the presence of Florizel and Perdita, and the *play* is
not issueless.

Just as important, Leontes's speech transforms the language of
the play. If the characteristic mode of discourse in Acts I–III.ii is
tragic and full of references to disease, becoming pastoral and
healthful in Act IV, the distinctive mode of speech in Act V is sacred and prepares the play for its version of romance hierophany. I
do not wish to belabor this point, but I think it is apparent that
Leontes's speech raises the prior issues of the play into a sacred,
which is not to say Christian, dimension. The issue of disease, for
example, is purged by the presence of Florizel and Perdita. Polixenes is now called a "holy father" who is "sacred," and against
whom Leontes has committed a "sin." Moreover, Leontes invokes
the "blessed gods" and the "heavens." This sense of the sacred, as
the penultimate experience of romance, is pushed still further in
V.ii which is a scene as unusual as III.iii. Leontes and Perdita are re-

united in this scene, but Shakespeare chooses not to allow the audience to witness the meeting, even though that reunion would satisfy the apparent conditions of the oracle of Apollo. Rather, the reunion is reported to us in a form of language that elevates strictly human activities into emblems or gestures of sacred experience, just as the "natural" conclusion of the play (the discovery of Perdita, the lost heir) is supplanted by the miraculous recovery of Hermione, which, as Brian Cosgrove has noted, "no reference to the cyclical pattern can account for."[13]

The design of V.ii, as it relates to the issue of children, seems to refer back to a remark that Paulina makes in II.ii. Speaking of the then diseased Leontes and the possible effect the presentation of the baby Perdita might have on him, Paulina says:

> We do not know
> How he may soften at the sight o' th' child;
> The silence often of pure innocence
> Persuades when speaking fails. (II.ii.37-40)

In V.ii we see how clearly the issue of children has been transformed from the tragedy of Acts I–III. Leontes does soften at the sight of "pure innocence" (Perdita, whom he earlier called a "female bastard"), but no less important, and perhaps more interesting, this scene reports the silence of innocence through the failure of speech, perhaps because it was speech, above all, that set off the tragedy of Act I (e.g., "Tongue-tied, our Queen? Speak you" (I.ii.27).

Hearing of the reunion of father and daughter, Autolycus tells the First Gentleman: "I would most gladly know the issue of it" (V.ii.8). The issue he hears about is the outcome of the distinctively sacred experience of romance, which exhausts the conventional resources of language. We are told, for example, that during the reunion "there was speech in their dumbness, language in their very gesture; they look'd as they had heard of a world ransom'd, or one destroy'd" (13-15). The reunion, moreover, was "a sight which was to be seen, cannot be spoken of" (42-43), the encounter "lames report to follow it, and undoes description to do it" (57-58), and we are told, "Every wink of an eye some new grace will be born" (110-11). This scene accomplishes the purgation of prior sorrow through present joy, even as it preserves our awareness of both the destructive past and the regenerative present. The wisest beholder, we are told, "could not say if th' importance were joy or sorrow, but in the extremity of the one it must needs be" (17-19); the King is ready to "leap out of himself for joy of his found daughter, as if that joy were now become a loss" (49-51); and the Third Gentleman refers to "the noble combat that 'twixt joy and sorrow was fought in Paulina!" (72-74). This purgation thus draws heavily on the past, but it is only dramatically consummated through the emblematic gestures of the birth of grace in V.iii, which is the final trial not only of the powers of romance to incorporate tragedy, but of the audience's ability to participate in the essentially sacred experience of romance that exists beyond tragedy.

When Leontes sees the statue of Hermione in V.iii he not only describes the experience of romance, but he speaks the language of romance. Like the audience, who also believes Hermione to be dead, Leontes attempts to express the wonder that is beyond tragedy. And though one could backtrack and argue that Hermione was alive all the time and that Paulina knew it, the initial and lasting effect of this scene is hierophanic; it is felt to be a manifestation of the sacred. Though realists might want to treat the play's resolution as the exclusive product of human agency—namely, Paulina's endeavors—everything in the scene is calculated to prevent characters, and I would say the audience, from raising such apparently irrelevant questions. Leontes himself suggests that we should "Let be, let be," and "Let't alone" (V.iii.61, 73). Moreover, if V.ii reports the silence of innocence, this scene enacts that silence. What Paulina does with the statue is conjure all the prior issues of the play—she speaks with an incantatory effect—in order to work Leontes, the source of the play's tragedy, into a state of mind that is the experience of romance. That state of mind is one of reverence, awe, and wonder, where the capacity to believe supplants the irritable reaching after fact that is associated with reason. The presence of the statue both purges and illumines the diverse issues of the play as we can see in Leontes's ever-widening responses:

> I am asham'd; does not the stone rebuke me
> For being more stone than it? O royal piece,
> There's magic in thy majesty, which has
> My evils conjur'd to remembrance.
>
> O sweet Paulina,
> Make me to think so twenty years together!
> No settled sense of the world can match
> The pleasure of that madness. (V.iii.37-40, 70-73)

And when Paulina says to Leontes, "I could afflict you farther," Leontes responds, "Do, Paulina; / For this affliction has a taste as sweet / As any cordial comfort" (75-77).

In these speeches Leontes quickly rehearses and regathers all the prior issues of the play. The sense of the play's tragic backdrop is "conjured to remembrance," at the same time that the tragedy is reversed by rejoining past time—"twenty years"—with present experience. Similarly, the art of the statue, like the art of the play, absorbs the varied stages and experiences of the play. Paulina, in purging the past illness of the play, performs a new "affliction" (an antidote, as it were) which, unlike Leontes's past disease, is at once healthful, lawful, and holy. Leontes is "transported," to use Paulina's term, at least twenty years back, and possibly much further. I say much further because Act V is dotted with references to "old tales"[14] (like a winter's tale) that may allude to Gower's notion in *Pericles—Et bonum quo antiquius eo melius*—which expresses, as I earlier suggested, one facet of romance's use of reversible time. Just as important, this projection back into time elicits a present experience of eternal time where the magic of Romano's art is as "Lawful as eating" (V.iii.111), just as Hermione's actions, Paulina later tells us, "shall be holy, as / You hear my spell is lawful" (V.iii.104-5).

The mentioning of law points to the most important issue of the play—the trial between the vying forces of tragedy and romance—

and it also demonstrates Shakespeare's conscious defiance of the conventional laws of "realistic" drama. [15] Somewhat reminiscent of the movement in *Pericles* from analogy, or mimetic art, to identity, or archetype and emblem, the play leads us to see that the statue itself, like the play, is not just like, but finally is, the moving image of eternity. Just as Time in IV.i declares that "it is in my pow'r / To o'erthrow law, and in one self-born hour / To plant and o'erwhelm custom" (IV.i.7-9), so we are later told that Julio Romano "had he himself eternity and could put breath into his work, would beguile Nature of her custom" (V.ii.97-99). This identification of art and nature in a union with Eternity is ultimately posed as a test for the characters and the audience, a test wherein we are required to abandon our ordinary sense of nature, law, and custom—the sources of discrepant awareness in *Cymbeline*—in order to awaken our faith, which is *the* experience of romance. Paulina states this test in such a way that it directly challenges our ability to experience the unique vision of Shakespeare's romances:

> It is requir'd
> You do awake your faith. Then, all stand still.
> On; those that think it is unlawful business
> I am about, let them depart. (V.iii.94-97)

Taken as an analogue to Shakespeare's romances, as well as an embodiment of the dramatic procedure of *The Winter's Tale,* Paulina's speech asserts the root experience of Shakespeare's romances, and Leontes becomes the supreme example of that experience. Our faith can only be awakened to the extent that we are willing to believe that time is reversible, that this process of reversibility is the experience of time as the moving image of Eternity, and that by virtue of this reversibility all human experience, as well as the customary forms of drama, can be absorbed into an experience beyond tragedy. Paulina's speech separates the faithful from the faithless. The faithful are emotionally moved, physically still, and content, to use Leontes's word. The faithless—those who regard the statue

scene as "unlawful business"—are emotionally reserved, intellec-
tually skeptical, and thus asked to depart.

In its celebration of "unlawfulness" *The Winter's Tale* is Shakespeare's most defiant romance. It is defiant in its use of time, in its
absorptive structure, and in its contempt for what passes for law
and custom; and this defiance is the final, all-embracing issue of the
play. The sixteen-year gap in time, the seacoast of Bohemia, the
character called Time, the sudden revelation that Hermione is alive,
and the union of art and nature—these are all examples of the play's
open defiance of law, in that they are designed to challenge our ability to experience romance.

The moment Hermione embraces Leontes we are startled, for we
have not been forewarned that she is alive. We have been led to believe that we know what is happening. Rather paradoxically, we
now believe Hermione is alive because we thought she was dead,
and we thus feel, like Leontes, that we have witnessed a miracle:
Shakespeare's "fine chisel" has "cut breath" (V.iii.78-79). When
Leontes says to Paulina

> What you can make her do,
> I am content to look on; what to speak,
> I am content to hear; for 'tis as easy
> To make her speak as move (91-94)

he is not speaking just for himself, but for our extraordinary experience of this play's conjuring of romance. No less appropriately,
Hermione's last words—"I have preserv'd / Myself to see the issue"
(127-28)—expresses both her symbolic significance and the play's
remarkable powers. The ultimate issue of the play, we see through
Hermione, is the ability of romance to regenerate life by proceeding
beyond tragedy.

SIX

Prospero's Art
and the Descent
of Romance

In the last chapter I argued that *The Winter's Tale* is marked by defiance, meaning that throughout the play Shakespeare is apparently quite willing to do implausible things. That willingness to challenge conventional notions of reality, including the audience's dependence on rational explanations, is best represented by the statue scene in V.iii. In a sense, this scene is the high point of Shakespearean romance, if we understand "high point" as a metaphor for a peak moment of imaginative experience. This experience, however, is the product of a dramatic process which initially posits a realistic situation, Leontes's tragic jealousy, and then proceeds to recycle and incorporate this situation, first through pastoral comedy in Act III.iii and Act IV, and then on into romance in Act V. More important, though, the dramatic process of *The Winter's Tale* may be regarded as a progressive elevation of the audience's awareness and experience. As *The Winter's Tale* moves both onward, through reversible time and its absorptive structure, and upward, as it were, toward hierophany, it replaces the process of reason with an ineffable sense of wonder which, in Paulina's words, is designed to awaken the characters' and audience's experience of faith.

The Tempest is not marked by such an imaginative ascent to the hierophanic experience of romance. Though there is a sense in which *The Tempest* is "the logical conclusion of the integrating process that produced *The Winter's Tale*,"[1] it is important to note that this play, unlike *The Winter's Tale,* enacts the imaginative descent of the experience of romance into areas more accessible to reason. The descending process continues in *Henry VIII*, where the experience of romance becomes fully rooted in history.[2] There are several ways that this process of descent appears in *The Tempest*, and perhaps the best means of stating my approach to the play is to revert to the paradoxical thesis that Prospero's art performs the dissolution of art in such a way that the imaginative representation or fiction of romance becomes, for the characters and the audience, the actual experience or fact of romance. I shall deal with this paradox by asking two general questions of the play: how and why does Prospero's dissolution of the art of romance yield the experience of romance?

As a preliminary move toward answering these questions, I first need to establish the presence of the defining attributes of Shakespearean romance—namely, an essential tragic backdrop, the absorption of the tragedy, and the culminating hierophanic moment which manifests the sacred experience of faith. As I observed earlier, the sense of wonder at the conclusion of *The Winter's Tale* is not repeated in *The Tempest*, partly because the latter play is more explicitly deliberate, as opposed to defiant, in its dramatic procedures. Indeed, one might say that when Miranda exclaims, "O brave new world / That has such people in't'" (V.i.183-84), she is speaking in the same language of wonder and amazement characteristic of Leontes's speech at the end of *The Winter's Tale*—e.g., "If this be magic, let it be an art / Lawful as eating." But the language and action of *The Tempest* are more often akin to Prospero's rejoinder, "'Tis new to thee," with the clear implication that Prospero, like *The Tempest*, is not easily susceptible to an uninspected sense of wonder.

The world of *The Tempest*, which is both the stage and the performance of Prospero's art, is both old and new, both real and imagined, and because it is both simultaneously, the play enacts different uses of time and absorption. The twelve-year gap in time, unlike the passage of sixteen years in *The Winter's Tale*, precedes the opening of the play, and this permits us to view *The Tempest* as an epilogue to a past tragic action in Milan, as Prospero's absorption in the present of that past action, and as a prologue, no longer controlled by Prospero's art, to the future actions of the characters on their return to Milan. Viewed as an epilogue to the time of twelve years past, the play, through Prospero's art, explores the idea that romance, in its absorption of tragedy and its use of reversible time, presents a dramatic and experiential realm beyond the seeming absolute close of tragedy. In contrast to tragedy, this play presents a number of characters with a second chance—a "second time" in the words of *Pericles*. This second time, paradoxically, is "new" time for Ferdinand and Miranda, and this is why they are so crucial to Prospero's performance of romance; but it is "old" time—that is, a possible regeneration in the present of the past—for Prospero, Alonso, Antonio, and Sebastian.

Speaking from the view of "new" time, Ferdinand says of Miranda:

> She
> Is daughter to this famous Duke of Milan,
> Of whom so often I have heard renown,
> But never saw before; of whom I have
> Receiv'd a second life; and second father
> This lady makes him to me. (V.i.191-96)

He has only heard of Prospero in the past; and now, during the play he sees him and receives a second life. Gonzalo, on the other hand, expresses a more comprehensive view of past and present time, but he formulates his experience in the language of "high" romance which is not to be identified with the rigor of Prospero's art. Summing up the plot of the play, especially its use of the absorption of tragedy through reversible time, Gonzalo exclaims:

> Was Milan thrust from Milan, that his issue
> Should become Kings of Naples? O, rejoice
> Beyond a common joy, and set it down
> With gold on lasting pillars: in one voyage
> Did Claribel her husband find at Tunis,

And Ferdinand, her brother, found a wife
Where he himself was lost; Prospero his dukedom
In a poor isle; and all of us, ourselves,
When no man was his own. (V.i.205-13)

As an epilogue the play peers into "the dark backward and abysm of time" (I.ii.50), which past is associated with tragedy, and as a prologue it looks forward to a new time codified by the marriage of Ferdinand and Miranda. But the epilogue and prologue, respectively associated with past and future, also serve as brackets enclosing Prospero's present performance of the play and its peculiar emphasis on present time. Prospero teaches characters in the present about the past in order to prepare them, as well as himself, for the future; as Joan Hartwig has observed, "The action of the play primarily concerns the education of the characters to a comprehension of what their tragi-comic vision means."[3] But the descending process of *The Tempest* is also calculated to dissolve distinctions between fiction and fact, the imaginary and the real; and this process of dissolution is evident in the play's recurrent use of the word *now*.

When Prospero tells Miranda that "thou must now know farther" (I.ii.33), that "The hour's now come, / The very minute bids thee open thine ear" (I.ii.36-37), when he opens Act V saying "Now does my project gather to a head," and when he declares in the Epilogue, "Now my charms are all o'erthrown / . . . Now I want / Spirits to enforce, art to enchant," he is addressing both the characters within the play and the audience without, at the same time that he is dissolving his art to affirm the immediacy of the play's experience. The repeated use of "now" joins our sense of virtual and real time, for every "now" within the play coincides with the audience's "now" outside the play.

Several commentators have observed how scrupulous Prospero is about asking what the time is, and it has also been suggested that the time within the play approximates the amount of time it takes to perform the play.[4] In Act I we are told that the time is at least two o'clock and that the play will occur during "The time 'twixt six and now" (I.ii.240), which is approximately the actual time of putting on the play. Similarly, we are reminded several times that the action of the play will take between three and four hours (III.i.21, V.i.136, 186, 223) and that it must conclude by suppertime (III.i.95, V.i.4). The effect of all this is to lock firmly into place the audience's sense of duration with the play's ostensible representation in such a way that the two are indistinguishable. But the play's peculiar use of time points in another direction as well—toward the unique character of Prospero's performance of romance. Because Prospero is, among other things, an artist who has staged a tempest within a play called *The Tempest*, it seems fair to assume that the play is also a kind of psychodrama with the characters and events of the play acting out facets of Prospero's mind.[5] At one point in Act IV, for instance, Prospero tells Ferdinand that the masque has been performed by "Spirits, which by mine art / I have from their confines call'd to enact / My present fancies" (IV.i.120-22). Viewed as psychodrama, the play is used by Prospero "To still my beating mind" (IV.i.163), which is to say his mind's tempestuous state is revealed through the characters and events of the play.[6] But instead of the customary hierophany of the romances, where some sacred presence externally manifests itself through an oracle, a dream, or a vision, *The Tempest* becomes its own hierophany. That is, the art, performance, and experience of the play become one and the same, and this is how Prospero performs his paradoxical intention of dissolving his art to elicit the fullest experience of romance.

A more specific way of seeing how this paradoxical process occurs is to examine what appears to be a deliberate pattern in the play, in which events are first viewed externally, then subjected to diverse interpretations based on the characters' past or present knowledge, then internalized as new states of awareness, and finally assimilated as a kind of communal experience. This process works in a manner similar to, though not identical with, the way discrepant awareness functions in *Cymbeline*. The story of Prospero's past life and present intentions is only partially known by the other characters. In fact, Prospero clusters all the characters save Ariel, who is the vehicle of his art, into three independent groups which are not collected until the end of the play.[7] These groups, which are continually dealt with separately, are, first, Ferdinand and Miranda; second, Alonso, Antonio, Sebastion, and Gonzalo; and third, Caliban, Stephano, and Trinculo. No one group sees the entire play, and thus it is, for example, that Alonso at the end of the play finds himself expressing amazement at events which only Prospero and the audience have fully experienced. Alonso observes, in a manner reminiscent of the end of *The Winter's Tale,* that

> This is as strange a maze as e'er men trod,
> And there is in this business more than nature
> Was ever conduct of, some oracle
> Must rectify our knowledge. (V.i.242-45)

Later, looking on Caliban, Alonso says, "This is a strange thing as e'er I look'd on" (290), and his last remark to Prospero is "I long / To hear the story of your life, which must / Take the ear strangely" (312-14).

But what is strange and unknown to Alonso is by now familiar and known to the audience. By the end of the play only the audience and Prospero share a complete knowledge of Prospero's story; as an oracle it is only our knowledge that Prospero has rectified. This helps to explain why the audience is addressed as participating and knowledgeable equals in the Epilogue, for only we have had the benefit of fully experiencing the deliberate pattern Prospero imposes on the respective groups of characters.

This pattern is the fourfold process beginning with the occurrence of a seemingly external event, followed by a character's initial interpretation of the event, then the character's subsequent internalization of the event's meaning as a new state of awareness, and finally a communal assimilation of the pattern as a bond of knowledge shared with Prospero. Only the audience and Prospero share a total knowledge of the process, and this is why Prospero promises to tell the characters his story (for us it would be a retelling) at the end of the play. Moreover, this sequential process is implied in the very title of the play. That is, *The Tempest* is an external event viewed by the characters as a storm and by the audience as a play. Seen as both a play and a storm, it is an analogue to, and a recapitulation and interpretation of, Prospero's tragic past: it separates the court, just as the court separated Prospero and Miranda from Milan, and it provides an interpretation of that separation. Furthermore, as a reflection of Prospero's mind *The Tempest* internalizes Prospero's new state of awareness resulting from his twelve-year separation; and, finally, the performance of *The Tempest,* understood either as a storm or as a play, assimilates these diverse experiences and pushes the play beyond the tragedy of twelve years past. Such a view of *The Tempest* as referring to both external events and internal states of mind is fully supported by the diverse meanings of the words "tempest," "wrack," and "rack" listed in the *OED,* by the one most frequently cited source of the play—William Strachey's *True Repertory of the Wracke*—and, most important, by the play's multiple uses of these terms. Indeed, there is no question that one effective way of producing this play would be to present it, and Prospero, in the character of a storm that slowly and systematically approaches clear weather.

Except for I.i, which is the physical storm, every scene in the first three acts is first marked by a response to the storm as an external event and then subjected to an interpretation based on past and present knowledge. Miranda's response and interpretation stand at the beginning of I.ii; Gonzalo's response and interpretation at the beginning of II.i; in II.ii it is Caliban who responds and interprets; at the opening of III.i it is Ferdinand; of III.ii Stephano, and of III.iii Gonzalo. Significantly, only in Acts IV and V does Prospero appear initially, and this is because here the characters begin to internalize, with Prospero's direct assistance, their experience of the external storm as a new state of awareness. Actually, even I.i presents a response to the storm, but it only intimates diverse interpretations of its meaning. Through some of the characters' earliest responses (especially those of the court), the play already begins to group the characters. The splitting of the boat, for example, intimates a moral split in the court. Gonzalo, who speaks for patience and prayers, aligns himself with Ferdinand and Alonso: "The King and Prince at prayers, let's assist them, / For our case is theirs" (I.i.54-55); but Sebastian, who is "out of patience" (55), responds

to Antonio's suggestion, "Let's all sink w' th' King," by saying,
'Let's take leave of him" (64), which, at least in retrospect, hints at
Sebastian's later willingness to assassinate Alonso.

But I.ii presents the audience with the first direct response and
interpretation of "The direful spectacle of the wrack" (I.ii.26)—the
"wrack" being both the external storm and shipwreck and the visible performance of Prospero's art. Miranda opens this scene by responding initially to the external appearance of the storm:

> If by your art, my dearest father, you have
> Put the wild waters in this roar, allay them.
> The sky it seems would pour down stinking pitch
> But that the sea, mounting to th' welkin's check,
> Dashes the fire out. Oh! I have suffered
> With those that I saw suffer. A brave vessel
> (Who had, no doubt, some noble creature in her)
> Dash'd all to pieces! (1-8)

Miranda's response immediately provokes two actions which lead
her, and us, through a process of interpretation. The first action is
that she calls into question the nature of Prospero's art which, in
turn, leads to an examination of Prospero's past. Prospero at once
assures Miranda that his art is "safely ordered" (29), and that her
understanding of that art is dependent on her knowledge of his and
her past history. The external storm, in other words, is calculated
to "inform thee farther" (23), for "The hour's now come, / The
very minute bids thee ope thine ear" (36-37). The repeated use of
"now" in this first part of I.ii (the word appears in lines 85, 111,
120, 137, 169, 175, 179, 183) has the effect of bringing forward
Prospero's past not just into present recollection, but into the present safe ordering of his art. That is, his art will transmute the past
in the present in such a way that Miranda's brief gesture toward internalization of Prospero's "sea-sorrow" (170)—i.e., "I, not re-
memb'ring how I cried out then, / Will cry it o'er again. It is a
hint / That wrings mines eyes to't" (133-35)—becomes a model of
the effect Prospero's art is designed to elicit.

In a similar way Prospero in the same scene subjects Ariel, Caliban and Ferdinand to a test of their understanding of the storm, and this test has the effect of bringing forward past knowledge into the present. Ariel, the vehicle of Prospero's art, complains about further "toil," and attempts to challenge Prospero by reminding him of "what thou hast promis'd, / Which is not yet perform'd me" (I.ii.243-44). Such a response stimulates Prospero's recollection of the past: "Dost thou forget / From what a torment I did free thee?" (250-51); and Prospero goes on to relate another facet of his history—namely, how he freed Ariel from Sycorax. Interestingly, Ariel, like Prospero, had been imprisoned for "A dozen years" (279), which may imply that Ariel stands in relation to Sycorax in approximately the same way that Prospero stands in relation to Alonso and Antonio. After all, at the end of the play Prospero and Ariel are freed from a twelve-year imprisonment, and they go their separate ways. In any event, Ariel's tentative resistance, like Miranda's earlier questioning, leads to another affirmation of the purposes of Prospero's art—"It was mine art, / When I arriv'd and heard thee, that made gape / The pine, and let thee out" (291-93)— and Ariel duly submits, like Miranda, to the power of Prospero's intentions: "I will be correspondent to command / And do my spiriting gently" (297-98).

In this scene Prospero deliberately elicits a range of responses to the storm which is the overt manifestation of his art. After Ariel the next respondent is Caliban, whom Prospero addresses, "slave! Caliban! / Thou earth, thou! speak" (I.ii.313-14). What Caliban speaks is neither Miranda's innocence, nor Ariel's yearning for freedom, but a kind of clamorous malignity. He tells Prospero, "A south-west blow on ye, / And blister you all o'er" (323-24), which speech immediately associates Caliban's language with a pestilential wind. Though endowed by Miranda with language, which is the instrument of Prospero's art, Caliban's cursing—"The red-plague rid you / For learning me your language!" (364-65)—defines his response as the outer limit of Prospero's art, as an element which can be dominated but not transformed by it.

If we consider the following lines from Ariel's song in this scene—"Nothing of him that doth fade / But doth suffer a sea-change / Into something rich and strange" (I.ii.400-402)—we can see that the characters' responses are being measured against their capacity to undergo a "sea-change" which is the transforming power of Prospero's art. Unlike Caliban, who curses Prospero's vision, Ferdinand hears Ariel's music and responds appropriately: "This music crept by me upon the waters, / Allaying both their fury and my passion / With its sweet air" (392-94). Ferdinand's language demonstrates his response to, though not necessarily an understanding of, the way the external storm and his "father's wrack" may be allayed by Prospero's art. The "sweet air" that he refers to may be taken both as a reference to the wind of the storm and as a musical term, referring to Ariel's song and Prospero's art. But the point is that Ferdinand's response reveals that Prospero's art is able to assimilate both the external (the fury of the waters) and the internal (Ferdinand's grief).

Significantly, then, Ferdinand's last speech at the end of I.ii is a vivid example of the first three stages of the process I have been examining: that is, the events of the storm viewed externally, the initial interpretation of the storm, and the subsequent internalization of the storm as a new state of awareness. By the end of the scene, when Prospero declares "It works" (434), Ferdinand and Miranda have basically internalized the meaning and experience of Prospero's art, which is to say they no longer resist the strangeness of the "sea-change." Thus Ferdinand says:

> My spirits, as in a dream, are all bound up.
> My father's loss, the weakness which I feel,
> The wrack of all my friends, nor this man's threats
> To whom I am subdu'd, are but light to me,
> Might I but through my prison once a day
> Behold this maid. All corners else o' th' earth
> Let liberty make use of; space enough
> Have I in such a prison. (487-94)

The most important element of Ferdinand's response is his submission to the confines—the "space"—of Prospero's art. His experience and internalization of Prospero's art are "light" in at least two respects. Prospero's art has lightened the burden of his apparent grief; it has transmuted Ferdinand's external loss of his father and friends into a dreamlike state which eases the weight of his grief. At the same time, the light contrasts with the apparent darkness of the storm and its consequences. Through Miranda he beholds the light of Prospero's art, and that light is the romance experience that occurs beyond tragedy. Thus the space of Ferdinand's seeming confinement is, in fact, the space which in the fifth act Prospero circumscribes as a magic circle, or the safe ordering of Prospero's art. By the end of the first act, therefore, Ferdinand and Miranda, who are so central to Prospero's purposes, have abandoned their initial interpretation of the storm and have internalized the experience of Prospero's art. Miranda speaks for the essential distinction between external interpretation and internal understanding when at the end of this act she observes: "Be of comfort. / My father's of a better nature, sir, / Than he appears by speech" (496-98).

As we have seen, the whole of I.ii presents a spectrum of responses to the "direful spectacle of the wrack," and except for Caliban, the main characters—Ariel, Miranda, Ferdinand—have internalized the experience of Prospero's art as a "strange" state of awareness—a "sea-change." But the second act, from which Prospero is significantly absent, represents a counterresponse and resistance to the internalization of new states of awareness. Gonzalo opens the act by attempting to interpret the "wrack" as a strange and wonderful experience, and he attempts to continue the language of Ferdinand and Miranda in I.ii:

> Beseech you, sir, be merry. You have cause
> (So have we all) of joy; for our escape
> Is much beyond our loss. Our hint of woe
> Is common; every day some sailor's wife,
> The masters of some merchant, and the merchant
> Have just our theme of woe; but for the miracle,
> (I mean our preservation), few in millions

Can speak like us. Then wisely, good sir, weigh
Our sorrow with our comfort. (II.i.1-9)

Gonzalo's speech may date as far back as IV.vi in *King Lear* where
Edgar, telling his father "Thy life's a miracle," continues: "thou
happy father, / Think that the clearest gods, who make them honors / Of men's impossibilities, have preserved thee" (IV.vi.55, 72-
74). Like Edgar, Gonzalo in this speech wishes to transform apparent tragedy into an experience beyond tragedy. He denies the
"theme of woe" because it is "common," and he reaffirms the miracle of their preservation because "our escape / Is much beyond our
loss." Without Prospero's direct assistance, Gonzalo is clearly capable of internalizing the experience of romance, but I think the main
purpose of his speech is to set up an explicit standard in this scene,
against which the responses of Alonso, Antonio, Sebastian, Caliban, Stephano, and Trinculo are to be measured. By this I mean
that these various characters' ridicule of Gonzalo's vision defines
their resistance to Prospero's art of romance. Instead of sharing
Gonzalo's understanding of the "wrack" as an opportunity for new
experiences, a number of these characters misuse the wrack as an
opportunity to wreak further destruction and to replicate, rather
than go beyond, past tragedies.

Gonzalo, of course, may be obviously naïve in his utopian vision
of the island, and his enthusiasm is not to be mistaken for Prospero's careful deliberation. As Harry Levin reminds us, "The myth
of the golden age [in short, Gonzalo's point of view] is a nostalgic
statement of man's orientation in time, an attempt at transcending
history."[8] But Prospero, unlike Gonzalo, does not want to tran-
scend history; he wants his place back in history. Nevertheless, the
fact remains that throughout Act II Gonzalo's experience functions
as the antithesis to the court's egocentric response. Every time Gonzalo attempts to affirm something he is just as quickly ridiculed,
and that ridicule, as we can see in the following passages, is an im-
plicit resistance to Prospero's art:

> *Gonzalo.* Here is everything advantageous to life.
> *Antonio.* True, save means to live. (II.i.50-51)

Gonzalo. But the rariety of it is—which is indeed almost
   beyond credit—
Sebastian. As many vouch'd rarieties are. (59-61)

Antonio. What impossible matter will he make easy next?
                                                    (89-90)

Alonso. You cram these words into mine ears against
   The stomach of my sense. (107-8)

Alonso. Prithee no more; thou dost talk nothing to me. (171)

But if Gonzalo's vision is "nothing" to Alonso, Antonio, and Sebastian, it remains true that they, like Gonzalo, have their own vision, though it is entirely rooted in the past and, indeed, replicates
the past.

To put it another way, where Gonzalo sees the storm and shipwreck as an opportunity for new experiences, the remaining characters in Act II respond to the storm by plotting further acts of devas-
tation which repeat the tragedy of twelve years past. Antonio,
clearly echoing what he did to Prospero twelve years before, turns
to Sebastian and says, "My strong imagination sees a crown / Drop-
ping upon thy head" (II.i.208-9). Their intentions are further distinguished from Prospero's performance when Antonio agrees that
he and Sebastian will "perform an act / Whereof what's past is prologue, what to come, / In yours and my discharge" (252-54).
Shakespeare so carefully and artfully distinguishes their response to
the storm from Gonzalo's that he aligns them, imagistically, with a
perverse internalization of "sea-change."

   Sebastian.   Well; I am standing water.
   Antonio. I'll teach you how to flow.
   Sebastian.   Do so. To ebb
      Hereditary sloth instructs me.
   Antonio.   O!
      If you but knew how you the purpose cherish
      Whiles thus you mock it! how, in stripping it,
      You more invest it! Ebbing men, indeed,

Most often do so near the bottom run
By their own fear or sloth. (221-28)

Furthermore, in II.ii Shakespeare again reverts to another grotesque internalization of ebbing and flowing, only ths time it appears in the form of "celestial liquor." The stage direction to II.ii
reads "A noise of thunder heard," and Caliban's initial response
demonstrates his distinctive attitude to the weather: "All the infec-
tions that the sun sucks up / From bogs, fens, flats, on Prosper fall,
and make him / By inch-meal a disease!" (II.ii.1-3). But the more
fascinating and grotesquely humorous response to the storm is
Trinculo's association of it, not just with water, but with alcohol.
He says,

Yond same black cloud,
Yond huge one, looks like a foul bumbard that would shed
his liquor. If it should thunder as it did before, I know not
where to hide my head. Yond same cloud cannot choose but
fall by pailfuls. (20-24)

Throughout the remainder of the scene Shakespeare presents several
variations on the idea of the ebbing and flowing of alcohol.
Stephano uses his wine as an apparent solution to Caliban's "fit"
(73ff.), and he even suggests to Caliban, in a mocking version of
Miranda's earlier remark to Caliban—"I endowed thy purposes / With words that made them known" (357-58)—that his
wine "is that which will give language to you, cat" (83). Moreover, we learn that Stephano "escaped upon a butt of sack"
(121),—a case of alcohol as salvation—and Stephano twice refers to
his own bottle (130, 142) as "the book," which is a clear mockery
of Prospero's high regard for books.

But perhaps the clearest example of how this scene presents an
egocentric resistance to Prospero's vision is in the implied comparison of Miranda's initial response to Ferdinand and Caliban's initial
estimation of Stephano and Trinculo. Both scenes draw on the same
use of language, though for widely differing purposes. On first seeing Ferdinand, Miranda asks,

What, is't a spirit?
Lord, how it looks about! Believe me, sir,
It carries a brave form. But 'tis a spirit.

.   .   .   .

I might call him
A thing divine, for nothing natural
I ever saw so noble. (410-12, 418-20)

To Ferdinand's query, "My prime request, / Which I do last pronounce, is (O you wonder!) / If you be maid, or no?" (I.ii.426-28),
Miranda appropriately responds: "No wonder, sir, / But certainly a
maid" (428-29). The language of Caliban's response to Stephano
and Trinculo duplicates the language of Ferdinand and Miranda by
way of comic exaggeration. In an aside Caliban assumes Stephano
and Trinculo to be "fine things, and if they be not sprites. / That's
a brave god, and bears celestial liquor. / I will kneel to him"
(II.ii.16-18). Caliban subsequently asks them, "Hast thou not
dropp'd from heaven?" (II.ii.137), and he then pledges himself to
them as gods: "A plague upon the tyrant that I serve! / I'll bear
him no more sticks, but follow thee, / Thou wondrous man" (162-
64).

As we have seen, the whole of Act II is based on antithetical responses. Alonso, Antonio, and Sebastian resist Gonzalo, who functions as a surrogate for Prospero's vision; and Caliban undermines
the language of Ferdinand and Miranda. The key dramatic point
seems to be that, in the absence of Prospero, only Gonzalo is capable of internalizing the affirmative meaning of the storm, whereas
the response of the other characters is based exclusively on the replication of past actions. Like Caliban, Sebastian and Antonio seek "a
new master" (II.ii.185), but their version of the "new" is really a
perverse continuation of the old—that is, the displacement of legitimate authority, as in twelve years past.

Act III presents the same range of responses seen in Acts I and II,
but the groups of characters are now at various stages of awareness.
If we apply the three stages I earlier mentioned of the external
storm, the initial interpretation, and the subsequent internalization

of new experiences, I think we can see that the three scenes of Act III place the characters along a spectrum of responses to Prospero's art. Whereas Caliban in II.ii wishes to free himself from laboring for Prospero, and whereas his understanding of that labor is purely external, Act III opens with Ferdinand bearing a log and explaining his internal understanding of what the labor signifies:

> There be some sports are painful, and their labor
> Delight in them [sets] off; some kinds of baseness
> Are nobly undergone! and most poor matters
> Point to rich ends. This my mean task
> Would be as heavy to me as odious, but
> The mistress which I serve quickens what's dead,
> And makes my labors pleasures. (III.i.1-7)

The several paradoxes of this passage, as also in III.i.33-34, 88-89, show how Ferdinand has internalized the external events, and his particular use of paradox serves as the linguistic analogue to the complex vision of Prospero's art. Because Ferdinand understands that "poor matters / Point to rich ends" (Gonzalo believes this as well), and because he has experienced how Miranda—really Prospero— quickens what's dead, he is at once lifted beyond apparent tragedy and beyond a purely egocentric view of himself and the events of the storm. Thus Prospero, in an aside, transforms the external elements of the storm, thereby exemplifying the process of internalization, when he declares about Ferdinand and Miranda: "Heavens rain grace / On that which breeds between 'em" (III.i.75-76).

But if the heavens "rain grace" on Ferdinand and Miranda, there is nothing but bad weather ahead in III.ii and III.iii. Once again the Caliban-Stephano-Trinculo plot is defined against the grace of Ferdinand and Miranda. While Ferdinand and Miranda, for all intents and purposes, are betrothed in III.i, Caliban and Stephano plan the rape of Miranda in another replication of a past action. In the same way, of course, they also plot revenge against Prospero and assume that Stephano and Miranda will be the new king and queen

(III.ii.107). Perhaps what measures the distance between Ferdinand's internalization of Prospero's vision and Caliban's cloudy understanding may be seen in a speech by Caliban which seems to echo Ferdinand's opening speech in III.i. Like Ferdinand, Caliban is sensitive to the strangeness of the island, and by implication the performance of Prospero's art, but he cannot internalize its meaning. Caliban tells an insensitive Stephano:

> Be not afeard, the isle is full of noises,
> Sounds, and sweet airs, that give delight and hurt not.
> Sometimes a thousand twangling instruments
> Will hum about mine ears; and sometimes voices,
> That if I then had wak'd after long sleep,
> Will make me sleep again, and then in dreaming,
> The clouds methought would open, and show riches
> Ready to drop upon me, that when I wak'd
> I cried to dream again. (III.ii.135-43)

Where the heavens do "rain grace" on Ferdinand and Miranda, they are only "Ready to drop" riches on Caliban because his understanding of Prospero's vision exists purely at the level of a dream. Indeed, his understanding of Prospero is so limited that this may be why (though I would not insist on it) Caliban earlier tells Stephano to kill Prospero now because "'tis a custom with him / I' th' afternoon to sleep" (III.ii.87-88); whereas Miranda in the preceding scene tells Ferdinand, "My father / Is hard at study; pray now rest yourself; / He's safe for these three hours" (III.i.19-21). Miranda knows better than to think that Prospero and his vision are so easily seduced by sleep and dreams.

In III.iii, however, we do see that the court, like Caliban, is seduced by illusion and that this susceptibility to illusion is a measure of their desperation. For the first time in the play Prospero provides the court with an interpretation of the external events, and he does so in a way that taunts their egocentric preoccupation with replicating the past. Although Alonso believes "The best is past" (III.iii.51), the main purposes of the illusory banquet is to remind

the court, excluding Gonzalo, of past sin (53), to indicate the
storm's symbolic purpose ("The pow'rs, delaying not forgetting),
have / Incens'd the seas and shores" (73-74), and to signify that
only "heart's sorrow" will produce "a clear life ensuing" (81-82).
Though Ariel's interpretation of the storm comes from the outside—it is not an interpretation that the court initiates—nevertheless, by the end of the scene Alonso, with Ariel's help, has internalized an understanding of what the storm means, as we can see in his
concluding speech:

> Methought the billows spoke, and told me of it;
> The winds did sing it to me, and the thunder,
> That deep and dreadful organ-pipe, pronounc'd
> The name of Prospero; it did base my trespass. (96-99)

In other words, the storm exemplifies the court's guilt, even as it
offers an opportunity for repentance. From this point on, Prospero
concentrates exclusively on the present and future by externally dissolving the storm and internally dissolving his art.

   As I observed much earlier in this chapter, the first three acts of
The Tempest open with a number of characters responding to and
interpreting the meaning of the storm. These responses and initial
interpretations are divided among groups of characters, and these
groups mark various stages of understanding. By the end of Act II
Ferdinand, Miranda, and perhaps Gonzalo are full, if not knowledgeable participants, in Prospero's vision. On the other hand, the
court understands only what the storm means in relation to the
past; theirs is a tragic understanding. And Caliban, Stephano, and
Trinculo are locked into their drunken dream of power. In Acts IV
and V Prospero rises to a surface understanding, emerges from the
storm to bring clear weather, and illuminates the meaning of his vision. He takes what formerly appeared externally, and what was
viewed as a product of supernatural power, and attempts to implant
it in the characters' natural understanding. But paradoxically in
order to give occasion for a full assimilation of the experience of romance he must perform the most daring—in that it involves the

most risk—action of the play: the public dissolution of his art into a "chronicle of day by day" (V.i.163).

Acts IV and V both engage in the dissolution of art, and Prospero once more is visibly at the center of the play's activities. Moreover, each act focuses on a central external event as a way of heightening the appearance of Prospero's art, and then Prospero dissolves that event in such a way that peak imaginative experiences descend to a more accessible form of understanding. It is important to understand, however, that when I refer to the dissolution of Prospero's art, I do not mean to suggest that he rejects his art. Rather, the dissolution is done to accomplish an assimilation of all the play's prior actions into an experience that is immediate, communal, and historical. The dissolution marks Prospero's final attempt to assimilate in his own person the total meaning of the various experiences the characters and audience have undergone.

For example, the masque in Act IV performs various functions in relation to Prospero's past, present, and future. We have seen earlier that Ferdinand and Miranda are the first group of characters to accede to Prospero's vision—they have internalized the awareness that all Prospero's "vexations / Were but my trials of thy love" (IV.i.5-6). Thus the masque is performed solely on their behalf. The other characters never see the masque; the closest they come to the performance is the chess game in Act V. As a "vanity of mine art," Prospero's masque is a very private celebration of the betrothal of Ferdinand and Miranda, and it is designed to reinforce the virtue of chastity.[9] At the same time, however, the visible appearance of the masque also projects a transformation of the external tempest, for what in the first three acts appeared as a storm now looks like a rainbow which is at once beautiful and evanescent. Visually, the presence of Iris, goddess of the rainbow, establishes Prospero's covenant, if you will, with Ferdinand and Miranda after the deluge of the tempest.[10] Nevertheless, Prospero, in what is sometimes regarded as an interpretive crux, breaks off the masque at precisely the point where Ferdinand begins to associate its vision with "Paradise" (IV.i.124).

If we inspect the sequence of events in which first the peak expe-

rience of the masque is established and then its effects are suddenly
disrupted, I think we can understand how and why Prospero must
dissolve his art. The process of descent of romance, which *The Tempest* enacts, begins in Act IV when Ferdinand responds to the
masque in a manner reminiscent of the statue scene in *The Winter's
Tale.* Ferdinand refers to the masque as "a most majestic vision"
(IV.i.118), and he subsequently exclaims "Let me live here
ever; / So rare a wond'red father and a wise / Makes this place Paradise" (122-24). Fifteen lines later Prospero, in an aside, recalls the
"foul conspiracy / Of the beast Caliban and his confederates," and
he then speaks his famous elegiac speech to the concerned Ferdinand:

> You do look, my son, in a mov'd sort,
> As if you were dismay'd; be cheerful, sir.
> Our revels now are ended. These our actors,
> (As I foretold you) were all spirits, and
> Are melted into air, into thin air,
> And like the baseless fabric of this vision,
> The cloud-capp'd tow'rs, the gorgeous palaces,
> The solemn temples, the great globe itself,
> Yea, all which it inherit, shall dissolve,
> And like this insubstantial pageant faded
> Leave not a rack behind. We are such stuff
> As dreams are made on; and our little life
> Is rounded with a sleep. (146-58)

The surrounding context of this speech of dissolution suggests not
the invalidity of Prospero's masque, but the impossibility of sustain-
ing its vision for a prolonged period of time. The masque may suggest the experience of paradise, but one cannot, as Ferdinand
wishes, "live here ever!" To attempt to sustain such a vision, in
fact, would replicate Prospero's past preoccupation with the supernatural which cost him his dukedom twelve years before. Such an
awareness may be the reason Prospero suddenly remembers Caliban's "foul conspiracy," for it was at the time of Prospero's peak

interest in magical visions that his throne was usurped. The point is that spirits will dissolve and "leave not a rack behind"—they are as evanescent as a rainbow—but Prospero is quite determined to leave much more than a "rack" (or "wrack") behind.

Indeed, Prospero's speech implies a necessary distinction between form and substance, or between appearance and intention. When Ferdinand asks Prospero, "May I be bold / To think these spirits?" (119-20), he responds, "Spirits, which by mine art / I have from their confines called to enact / My present fancies" (120-22). Throughout his speech to Ferdinand, Prospero characterizes only the vehicle and appearance of the masque as "insubstantial": he does not, like Ferdinand, mistake the vehicle of art for the purpose of that art. Prospero understands his spiritual art as an extension of mind and body, and not merely as an expression of imagination. Though Marsh contends that "Prospero would like man to be all mind,"[11] I believe Prospero's recollection of Caliban is a necessary element in the play's process of descent, a process whose fullest meaning depends on an assimilation of all that is body. In this respect, I agree with Kermode that "Caliban is the ground of the play."[12] Caliban may be "A devil, a born devil, on whose Nature / Nurture can never stick" (188-89), but the nurture of Prospero's art is not just defined against, but is defined by, its acknowledgment of the body of humanity—e.g. "this thing of darkness [Caliban] I / Acknowledge mine" (V.i.275-76).

In contrast to the external absorption that occurs in the previous romances, where some external power (Diana, Apollo, Jupiter) resolves the play, in the fifth act of *The Tempest* Prospero himself provides an internal absorption and assimilation. Prospero's dissolution of art and his abandonment of magic are paradoxical because they deny an exclusively supernatural understanding of the play in order to dramatize Prospero's central gesture of faith—his return to the body of humanity. In rejecting the visible accoutrements of his art, Prospero emphatically demonstrates that the experience of romance is fundamentally human and accessible to a natural understanding, as opposed to being wholly dependent on external supernatural forces. Throughout Act V Prospero systematically distinguishes be-

tween the supernatural appearance of his art and the human design
which motivates that art. For example, early in Act V Ariel tells
Prospero, "Your charm so strongly works 'em, / That if you now
behold them, your affections / Would become tender" (V.i.17-19),
to which Prospero replies:

> Dost thou think so, spirit?
> *Ariel.* Mine would, sir, were I human.
> *Prospero.*   And mine shall.
>   Hast thou, which art but air, a touch, a feeling
>   Of their afflictions, and shall not myself,
>   One of their kind, that relish all as sharply
>   Passion as they, be kindlier mov'd than thou art?
>   Though with their high wrongs I am strook to th' quick,
>   Yet with my nobler reason, 'gainst my fury
>   Do I take part. The rarer action is
>   In virtue than in vengeance. They being penitent,
>   The sole drift of my purpose doth extend
>   Not a frown further. Go, release them, Ariel.
>   My charms I'll break, their senses I'll restore,
>   And they shall be themselves. (19-32)

Prospero here addresses Ariel as being "insubstantial," for Ariel,
like the spirits of the masque, is "but air." This time, though, the
purpose of the speech is far more explicit: namely, to establish that
Prospero, even in light of his supernatural powers, is finally "One
of their kind." Prospero again descends from his supernatural appearance and dissolves his art (Ariel being the primary vehicle of
that art); and he does so to reinforce his basic humanity. In fact, the
last two lines of this speech set up the sequence of events that gov-
erns the remainder of the play, but it is essential to realize that the
sequence applies to Prospero as well as to the other characters. Only
the dissolution of his "charms" will lead to the restoration of the
characters' "senses" and will enable them, along with Prospero, to
become "themselves."

The sequence I have mentioned is both set up and initiated in the longest continuous speech of the play (V.i.33-87). As in the elegiac speech following the masque, Prospero dissolves his art, but the meaning of this dissolution is far more comprehensive. Prospero abjures his "rough magic," saying that

> when I have requir'd
> Some heavenly music (which even now I do)
> To work mine end upon their senses that
> This airy charm is for, I'll break my staff,
> Bury it certain fadoms in the earth,
> And deeper than did ever plummet sound
> I'll drown my book. (51-57)

Quite revealingly, I think, Prospero's last lines echo Alonso's speech of maximum disillusionment when, on hearing Prospero's name in Act III, he concludes: "Therefore my son i' th' ooze is bedded; and / I'll seek him deeper than e'er plummet sounded, / And with him there lie mudded" (III.iii.100-102). The burial of Prospero's book, the dissolution of his art, restores the life of the body; the descent of the book represents the ascent of "sense"— Prospero speaks of their "rising senses" (V.i.66)—and by sense is meant both body and understanding. This process reverses the customary ascent to hierophany in the prior romances.

Perhaps more important, the descent and dissolution of Prospero's art also represent the time of maximum assimilation between what appeared, in the eyes of the court, to be an external tempest produced by supernatural power, and what is, finally, an internal tempest that conjoins external appearance with a basically internal and humanly comprehensible meaning. For instance, looking on the court Prospero says:

> Their understanding
> Begins to swell, and the approaching tide
> Will shortly fill the reasonable [shores]
> That now lie foul and muddy. (V.i.79-82)

This speech suggests that the tempest, as a storm and a play, enacts a condition of mind; it addresses the characters' senses through the vehicle of imagination, just as the nautical imagery that concludes the play,

> I'll deliver all,
> And promise you calm seas, auspicious gales,
> And sail so expeditious, that shall catch
> Your royal fleet far off (314-17)

refers not only to a safe voyage home, but to a projected state of mind beyond the tragedy of what the court and Prospero experienced as "the direful spectacle of the wrack."

But this is just one example of how Prospero establishes the descent of his vision into the senses of the characters. Another way that his dissolution of art produces a descent of romance is indicated by the lines, "I will discase me, and myself present / As I was sometime Milan" (V.i.85-86). That is, if the characters "shall be themselves," then it is only appropriate that Prospero should become himself, which is to say he will become fully human. Therefore, when he appears to Alonso as the "wrong'd Duke of Milan, Prospero," the first thing he does is to "embrace thy body" (109) and "embrace thine age" (121). His appeal to Alonso is physical, not spiritual, and natural, not supernatural. Such an appeal yields the sense of penitence that Prospero seeks to elicit, for Alonso responds:

> Thy pulse
> Beats as of flesh and blood; and since I saw thee,
> Th' affliction of my mind amends, with which
> I fear a madness held me. (113-16)

The essential paradox, then, of Prospero's dissolution of art is that it simultaneously enacts, from Prospero's point of view, the descent of romance, and from the vantage point of the court, the ascent of their experience of romance. The court rises to Prospero's descent. Both Prospero and the court move beyond tragedy to a "second time." But this movement is primarily physical for Prospero, dating back to his twelve-year separation from Milan, and primarily mental for the court, since they have been separated from one another for a mere three hours. The court continually seeks to elevate their experience of romance, to see it as a miraculous event, as we can see, for example, in their response to Ferdinand and Miranda playing chess:

> *Alonso.*   If this prove
> A vision of the island, one dear son
> Shall I twice lose.
> *Sebastian.* A most high miracle!
> *Ferdinand.* Though the seas threaten, they are merciful;
> I have cursed them without cause. [*Kneels*] (175-79)

Yet Prospero insists on the descent—the human accessibility and limitations—of that experience, for what is a "brave new world" to Ferdinand, Miranda, and the court is hardly a "vision of a new humanity" to Prospero.[13] Rather, it is "a chronicle of day by day, / Not a relation for a breakfast" (163-64).

Moreover, just as Prospero meets the characters in his own person, stripped of his supernatural appearance and power, so he meets the audience in the Epilogue as a person, declaring "what strength I have's mine own" (line 2). This, it seems to me, is the final and most comprehensive moment of Prospero's descent. The dissolution of Prospero's art maximizes the human accessibility of the play's meaning, for Prospero has removed every barrier, save that of human understanding, which might separate him from either the characters or the audience. Now lacking "Spirits to enforce, art to enchant," Prospero and the audience meet in their respective strengths. What began as an external tempest in the eyes of the characters, and as a stage play in the eyes of the audience, concludes as a "real" event now, in which the audience is asked to reproduce the prayer, mercy, and forgiveness that Prospero has enacted in the play. The Epilogue is Prospero's descent to the audience and his final gesture of faith. But that descent entails the audience's ascent to a reciprocal act of faith, for just as we "from crimes would pardon'd be," so our indulgence—our patient understanding—must set him free. For the last time Prospero breaks his charms to elicit the fundamentally human experience of romance.

SEVEN

History, Romance, and *Henry VIII*

Prospero's descent into history, signified by his desire to return to Milan and his method of accomplishing that end, represents not only a move beyond tragedy but an attempt to align the experience of romance much more closely with the audience's sense of "reality." Finally appearing in his own person, stripped of his supernatural powers, Prospero both is and enacts the absorptive power of Shakespearean romance. But where Prospero expresses a wish to return into history, *Henry VIII,* viewed as an extension of *The Tempest's* descending process, constitutes a historical version, if not a historical verification, of the literary experience of romance.

I am not the first person to suggest that *Henry VIII* is strongly related to the prior romances, and my basic approach is in part indebted to such critics as G. Wilson Knight, H. M. Richmond, Frances Yates, and R. A. Foakes. I am also aware of the apparently insoluble quarrel about the authorship of *Henry VIII,* a quarrel based entirely on internal evidence, and I have no hard data on which to argue convincingly that Shakespeare did, or did not, write the entire play. Even Samuel Schoenbaum, who holds the collaborationist view, has conceded that "the problem admits of no ultimate solution."[1] Nevertheless, I am inclined to agree with H. M. Richmond when he says about the authorship of *Henry VIII*: "Either we have here the culmination of Shakespeare's career, or a dramatist who understood Shakespeare's evolution of interest so well that he managed to complete the sequence by an insight denied to the master himself."[2]

Some of the recurrent romance devices that appear in *Henry VIII* are these: the use of trials (explicitly of four characters; implicitly, as in *The Winter's Tale,* of the audience's ability to believe the play's "chosen truth"), the association of women with chastity and divinity, the symbolic importance of the birth of a daughter, the presence of honest counselor figures, the pattern of fortunate falls, the emphasis on patience, the presence of hierophany and dependence on providential intrusions, the breakup and consolidation of royal families, and the pronounced emphasis on faith as the penultimate experience of romance. Many of these devices have been scrupulously noted by R. A. Foakes.[3] The devices, taken alone or collectively, suggest literary influence, but they may not bear directly on my contention that *Henry VIII* is at once an extension of the prior romances and a historical verification of the literary experience of romance.

What does relate directly to my argument is the clear presence of those structural characteristics which I have called the defining properties of Shakespearean romance. That is, *Henry VIII* employs a plot version of tragedy—really three tragedies (Buckingham, Wolsey, Katherine)—that subsequently incorporates the tragic loss of the previous generation. Moreover, the play's movement depends on the use of generic absorption; in this case the seemingly recalcitrant materials of history are absorbed by a providential interpretation of what these events symbolize. The prophetic mode in which Cranmer finally speaks certainly draws on the audience's ability to identify with the Age of Elizabeth. Furthermore, the final act clearly elicits a romance version of redemption, wherein the historical facts of the reign of Henry VIII are redeemed, particularly, by Cranmer's providential understanding of what the birth of Elizabeth signifies. But *Henry VIII* advances its use of romance devices one bold step further than the earlier romances by establishing a correlation between historical personages and romance conventions, and by pursuing a providential view of history (including the so-called Tudor Myth) supported by the Reformation and the rise of Protestantism associated with Cranmer and Elizabeth.

Such assertions, I will immediately concede, place a heavy load of meaning on what is generally regarded as a distinctly lightweight play. But at least they get out into the open what is the interpretive crux of the play—the relation between history and romance, or between the known facts of history and an essentially providential understanding of their symbolic import. There is a tension—possibly an irreconcilable opposition—between what the reader and the audience know about history and what the play attempts to do, and this tension is evident in recent criticism of the play. On the one hand, H. M. Richmond suggests that *Henry VIII* "alone seems to illustrate in plausible historical terms the application of the spirit in which *The Tempest* was written to the actual events of the English sixteenth century." Somewhat more specifically, G. Wilson Knight, who views *Henry VIII* as "Shakespeare's one explicitly Christian play," argues that we are "to feel British Protestantism rising in Cranmer, his advance contrasting with the fall of Wolsey, whose intrigues are partly to be associated with Rome." More recently, Frances Yates has observed that "in *Henry VIII*, we have the culmination of Foxian history with the throwing off of papal power in the name of the sacred majesty of the Monarch."⁴ Yates also revealingly mentions an illustration in Foxe's *Acts and Monuments*—the principal source of Act V—"which shows Henry seated on the throne of royal majesty, dismissing the papal representatives and honouring Cranmer, who holds the open Bible."⁵ In fact, the illustration shows Henry VIII with his feet on the pope, a gesture representative of the strongly anti-papist bent of the play.

If these views represent the strongest defense of the use of history in *Henry VIII*, the severest attack is that of Howard Felperin who argues:

> The "chosen truth" of this play is so much more "chosen" than "true" as to be quite incredible. Too much is censored out or glossed over. . . . For history, the mode in which the reality principle commands its fullest recognition, and romance, the mode in which it receives its freest treatment, are the poles of Shakespeare's imaginative universe and are irreconcilably opposed. . . . Whereas John of Gaunt eulogized En-

gland as an "other Eden, demi-paradise" in a history play that made clear he was voicing a wish rather than a fact, *Henry VIII* tries to present the thing itself and confuses the wish and the fact.[6]

Although I disagree with Felperin's assertion that history and romance are "the poles of Shakespeare's imaginative universe and are irreconcilably opposed," I think his statement locates the interpretive crux of the play. We have seen before how Shakespeare's romances can absorb divergent experiences and materials, but this is the first play I have examined which systematically attempts to absorb the known materials of history into the mode of romance. *Cymbeline* casts passing glances at English history, but it hardly commands the historical attention of *Henry VIII*. Certainly Felperin is right to suggest that the most intransigent materials for romance to absorb are the known facts of history, for history is indeed "the mode in which the reality principle commands its fullest recognition." Nevertheless, I have serious reservations about Felperin's conjunction of history and *the* reality principle, simply because by modern standards of historical verifiability a good deal of Holinshed, for instance, would have to be regarded, to borrow Felperin's later remarks, as a confusion of wish and fact. Henry Ansgar Kelly, has shown in abundant detail how Renaissance historiography deals less with what modern historians regard as fact because it translates fact as evidence of providential intervention in the affairs of man.[7] In other words, Renaissance historiography propounds myths—the Lancaster Myth, the York Myth, the Tudor Myth—but these myths are believed-fictions, or modes of historical observation, even if we moderns treat them with considerable skepticism. These myths constitute divergent but systematic interpretations of history, and perhaps most interestingly they are based on a symbolic understanding of what we call facts. As Kelly's study implies, there is ample precedent for believing that what Felperin regards as an irreconcilable opposition between history and romance is, in fact, an anachronistic distinction superimposed upon Renaissance materials by modern criticism.

To state it positively, considerable evidence in Renaissance historiography suggests that providential views of history are easily conjoined with the literary rise of romance because romance itself relies, as we have repeatedly seen, on providential interpretations and experiences. The literary device of hierophany, for example, could easily be linked with providential historiography, and this is precisely what *Henry VIII* does. The facts of Henry VIII's reign, as we moderns know them, are less important in the play than their symbolic meaning; as in Foxe's *Acts and Monuments,* we shall find that in Act V of *Henry VIII* "history and prophecy [are] in effect one continuing revelation of divine providence working upon the life of mankind."[8]

In several ways we can see that the dominant intention of *Henry VIII* conjoins the events of history with the conventions of romance in such a manner that the play presents a historical verification of the literary experience of romance. The first way is to examine the falls of Buckingham, Wolsey, and Katherine, all of which draw on Holinshed's *Chronicles.* The second way is to note the religious drive in the play which, albeit anachronistically, steadily implies and anticipates a turn away from Catholicism to the rise of Protestantism; this turn is evident not only within the play, but within the play's primary source for Cranmer's trial, Foxe's *Acts and Monuments.* The third way is to focus on how and why Cranmer, not Henry VIII, emerges in the last act as the primary spokesman for what the play means. It is my view that Cranmer's prophecy both consolidates and expresses the play's historical verification of the literary experience of romance.

We have seen throughout this study that Shakespeare's romances in varying ways elicit the unique movement of an experience beyond tragedy by first presenting the audience with one or more apparent tragedies. *Henry VIII* is no different in this respect, except that it dramatizes three apparent tragedies and the expectation of a fourth—Cranmer's, which is short-circuited. Indeed, the action of *Henry VIII*—somewhat like that of *The Winter's Tale*—may be envisioned as a diptych, a tragic half countered by a romance absorption of that tragedy. The events of the latter half provide a providential perspective for the events of Acts I–IV; and the function of Elizabeth's birth or Cranmer's prophecy is to provide a reappraisal, not a denial, of the tragic events that precede it.

If we concentrate on the falls of Buckingham, Wolsey, and Katherine, we can see that these events are dramatized through a double focus, wherein the ostensible facts of history are absorbed by a larger providential interpretation which is characteristic of the romances. For example, the question of Buckingham's treason (as a number of critics and editors have noted) is at best ambiguous, because Katherine, among others, doubts the credibility of the testimony against him. But the question of guilt or innocence seems much less important than the larger question, again posed by the Second Gentleman, dealing with Buckingham's response to having been found guilty of treason. The Second Gentleman asks, "After all this, how did he bear himself?" (II.i.30), and the remainder of the scene is entirely concerned with Buckingham's attitude to death, which is an attitude of "a most noble patience" (36).

The virtue of patience, which is a prominent characteristic of Shakespeare's romances, is traditionally associated with Christ's humility and it signals an individual's resignation to providential forces larger than individual destiny. In the romances this conception dates as far back as *Pericles,* where Marina is emblematically likened to "Patience gazing on kings' graves, and smiling / Extremity out of act" (V.i.138-39). If Buckingham does not smile "extremity out of act," he at least translates his individual fate into an instrument for reaffirming the power of providence where "Heaven has an end in all" (II.i.124). What is notable about Buckingham's fall, and quite characteristic of the play's remaining falls, is his ability to project his fate as part of a pattern of a larger destiny. That sense of destiny is distinguished by a spirit of faith, forgiveness, and charity, as we can see in the following lines:

> yet, heaven bear witness,
> And if I have a conscience, let it sink me,
> Even as the axe falls, if I be not faithful!
> The law I bear no malice for my death;

'T has done, upon the premises, but justice,
But those that sought it I could wish more Christians.
Be what they will, I heartily forgive 'em. (II.i.59-65)

Buckingham then reaffirms the very rule of Henry VIII which may
have victimized him:

Commend me to his Grace,
And if he speak of Buckingham, pray tell him
You met him half in heaven. My vows and prayers
Yet are the King's; and, till my soul forsake,
Shall cry for blessings on him. (86-90)

Even Wolsey, who is frequently likened to the devil, and who is
continually held responsible for the evil doings in the play, himself
achieves a moment of illumination where he, too, understands his
historical fate as an emblem of providential destiny. In addition, and
perhaps more peculiarly, Wolsey, as the supreme Catholic, is given
a turn of phrase that seems to anticipate the strongly Protestant
character of Act V. Among other things, Wolsey says at the moment of his fall:

Vain pomp and glory of this world, I hate ye!
I feel my heart new open'd. O how wretched
Is that poor man that hangs on princes' favors!
There is, betwixt that smile we would aspire to,
That sweet aspect of princes, and their ruin,
More pangs and fears than wars or women have;
And when he falls, he falls like Lucifer,
Never to hope again. (III.ii.365-72)

Then, after declaring, "The King has cur'd me, / I humbly thank
his Grace" (380-81), Wolsey addresses an important speech to
Cromwell:

Say, Wolsey, that once trod the ways of glory,
And sounded all the depths and shoals of honor,

Found thee a way, out of his wrack, to rise in;
A sure and safe one, though thy master miss'd it.
Mark but my fall, and that that ruined me:
Cromwell, I charge thee, fling away ambition!
By that sin fell the angels; how can man then
(The image of his Maker) hope to win by it?
Love thyself last, cherish those hearts that hate thee;
Corruption wins not more than honesty.
Still in thy right hand carry gentle peace
To silence envious tongues. Be just, and fear not;
Let all the ends thou aim'st at be thy country's,
Thy God's, and truth's; then if thou fall'st, O Cromwell,
Thou fall'st a blessed martyr. (435-49)

Wolsey's gnomic lines at once draw on the known materials of history and reinterpret them in a strongly providential and Protestant manner. Moreover, his lines show how the materials of history, including his own tragic fall, are translated and absorbed through the conventions of romance. For example, Wolsey as a Catholic utters a line taken straight out of the Anglican liturgy. As Richmond Noble has observed, the phrase "Vain pomp and glory of this world" is an explicit allusion to the sentence in the Anglican baptism service, "Dost thou forsake the devil and his works, the vain pomp and glory of this world"? This allusion has prompted R. A. Foakes to suggest, "No doubt the allusion is intended, for Wolsey learns in his fall to be a Christian."[9] No doubt, also, such an implication involves considerable historical distortion, but that distortion points to the basically Protestant intent of the play. In a sense, as Richmond Noble has suggested, Wolsey's first lines might be seen, in a double focus, as his fall as a Catholic and his implied baptism (his "heart new open'd") into the "truth" of Protestantism which is, ultimately, the "chosen truth" of the play.

But there is still more evidence in this scene that the tragic fall of Wolsey has been absorbed by a conjunction of religious Protestantism and the providential impulse of Shakespearean romance. In the second passage I have quoted, Wolsey's speech draws on the tempest imagery of the romances. Wolsey, who has "sounded the depths and shoals of honor," says that his own fall has found Cromwell "a way, out of [this]wrack, to rise in." This is an exact description of romance's movement beyond tragedy, and it may well echo one of the suggested sources of *The Tempest,* William Strachey's *True Repertory of the Wracke,* which pamphlet plays on the double movement of wrack and redemption. Wolsey's fall signals Cromwell's rise, and Cromwell's rise foretells Henry's break with Rome; for it was Cromwell, Shakespeare's immediate audience would likely know, who assisted Henry VIII "in his unprecedented claim to be Supreme Head of the Church of England, which was decreed by the Act of Supremacy in 1534."[10] Moreover, Wolsey's advice to Cromwell that he should "let all the ends thou aim'st at be thy country's, / Thy God's, and truth's" seems to consolidate what historically occurred through the Act of Supremacy, and what in this play culminates with the rise of Cranmer in Act V.

Historically, Cromwell may not have fallen as "a blessed martyr," but his rise out of Wolsey's "wrack" does associate the romances' tempest imagery with the subsequent historical emergence of the Church of England. Indeed in Act V, which draws heavily on Foxe's *Acts and Monuments,* we shall see that the tempest imagery of this play at least parallels, and may allude to, Foxe's exhortation to the Church of England now that it has escaped "the Babylonish captivity." The tempest imagery, as the following passage from Foxe demonstrates, refers both to church and state, and it subsequently represents the time of Cranmer's prophecy when "God shall be truly known" (V.iv.36):

> God has so placed us Englishmen here in one commonwealth, also in one church, as in one ship together, let us not mangle or divide the ship, which, being divided, perisheth; but every man serve with diligence and discretion in his order, wherein he is called.—they that sit at the helm keep well the point of the needle, to know how the ship goeth, and whither it should; whatsoever weather betideth, the needle, well touched with the stone of God's word, will never fail: such as

labor at the oars start for no tempest, but do what they can to keep from the rocks: likewise they which be in inferior rooms, take heed they move no sedition nor disturbance against the rowers and mariners. No storm so dangerous to a ship on the sea, as is discord and disorder in a weal public. . . . The God of peace, who hath power both of land and sea, reach forth his merciful hand to help them up that sink, to keep up them that stand, to still these winds and surging seas of discord and contention among us; that we, professing one Christ, may, in one unity of doctrine, gather ourselves into one ark or the true church together; where we, continuing steadfast in faith, may at the last luckily be conducted to the joyful point of our desired landing-place by his heavenly grace.[11]

This passage from Foxe provides a rationale for the absorption of the materials of history in *Henry VIII*, especially the tragic falls of Catholics, by certain romance conventions which are linked with the rise of Protestantism. Historically, Henry's break with Rome (he was excommunicated, along with Anne Bullen and Cranmer, in July of 1533) did not imply his conversion to Protestantism. To the contrary, as A. F. Pollard has prudently observed: "In spite of the store which he set upon his own private judgment, Protestant theology never made its way into Henry's heart or mind. He had abolished the Pope, but not Popery, wrote Bishop Hooper. It would be truer to say that he had taken the place of the Pope in the English Church, and substituted a Royal for a Roman Catholicism."[13] These are the facts of history, just as Henry's divorce (really annulment) historically marked his break with Rome. Still, if we keep in mind Muriel St. Clare Byrne's observation that *Henry VIII* "is a play about Tudor succession, by an Elizabethan" then we can see that the play's use of the Tudor Myth does not mark, as Felperin argues, "an interesting failure."[14] Rather, the Tudor Myth, conjoined with history in the Foxe tradition, supports the play's romance absorption of tragedy.

This romance absorption of historical tragedy may be seen in the fall of Katherine, the final tragedy of the play. Like Buckingham and Wolsey, Katherine undergoes a trial, but once again her historical fall elicits a providential interpretation.[15] The scene of her fall is so constructed that the known materials of history are shaped by the introduction of three romance conventions that are not present in the historical source of this scene, Holinshed's *Chronicles*. R. A. Foakes has noted that Griffith "is not mentioned in connection with [Katherine's] death in Holinshed, but he is named in relation to her trial." Second, Katherine's maid Patience is "wholly an invention,"[16] and there is no source in the *Chronicles* for Katherine's hierophanic vision in IV.ii. Clearly, then, the scene is less concerned with history than with a calculated dramatic impact; so the question arises, what are these romance conventions designed to do?

If we assume, as H. M. Richmond has argued, that "Katherine's character represents the norm against which we must measure the other characters,"[17] then I think her fall explicitly signals the play's subsequent absorption of tragedy. The introduction of several romance conventions reinforces this idea. Griffith, for instance, occupies the role of the loyal and wise counselor figure, continuing the tradition of Helicanus, Pisanio, Camillo, and Gonzalo. As Katherine says, Griffith is "an honest chronicler" (IV.ii.72) because he states both the strengths and weaknesses of Wolsey's character in such a way that Katherine concludes: "Whom I most hated living, thou has made me, / With thy religious truth and modesty, / Now in his ashes honor" (73-75). This change of estimate is in itself significant, for the fall of Katherine both absorbs and explains the fall of Wolsey, her hated enemy. Katherine wants to know how Wolsey died because "If well, he stepp'd before me happily / For my example" (10-11). Thus, it is the manner, not the fact, of his death that matters, and it is fascinating to watch how Katherine's fall in part echoes what Wolsey says at the moment of his fall. As a loyal counselor, Griffith performs the same role for Katherine that Cromwell does for Wolsey. Just as Katherine responds to Griffith as an "honest chronicler" who speaks with "religious truth and honesty," so Wolsey says to Cromwell: "I did not think to shed a tear / In all my miseries; but thou has forced me, / Out of thy honest truth" (III.ii.428-30). And just as Wolsey tells Cromwell, "I know myself now, and I feel within me / A peace above all earthly dignities, / A still and quiet conscience" (III.ii.378-80), so Shakespeare, through the vehicle of the character Patience (a clear romance emblem) and through the stage directions accompanying Katherine's vision, presents Katherine with a hierophany "*at which (as it were by inspiration) she makes (in her sleep) signs of rejoicing, and holdeth up her hands to heaven.*" In short, she is lifted out of tragedy.

These falls embody a romance absorption of historical tragedy, or a providential interpretation of historical events. The dramatic rhythm of the play is so designed that the audience is led to anticipate a fourth trial and fall—that of Cranmer. But before we look at Cranmer's trial, I wish to examine the relationship between the falls of Buckingham, Wolsey, and Katherine and the steady emergence of a Protestant ethos in the first four acts of the play. Such an examination is necessary not merely to demonstrate that the fifth act presents a historical confirmation of the literary experience of romance, but to counterbalance the critical view that the last act is in no way prepared for. Such a negative view has been most vigorously asserted by Peter Milward:

> In the fifth act, however, the play makes a complete *volte-face*; and the atmosphere of tragedy rolls away, with no accompanying change of character. . . . This is all quite out of harmony with the preceding acts, as shadow suddenly turns to light, tragedy ends in comedy, and tears are exchanged for laughter, without any justification in terms of character. . . . One can only suspect that the final act was left in the hands— for whatever reason—of an inferior dramatist, who was insufficiently aware of the master plan—whatever it may have been—and was chiefly intent on bringing the tragic events to a happy outcome, on the superficial model of Shakespeare's previous tragicomedies.[18]

Interestingly, Milward's criticism could be applied just as easily, and just as doubtfully, to *The Winter's Tale,* for there "the atmos-

phere of tragedy rolls away" quite abruptly at the end of III.ii.
What Milward's criticism really attests to is the exhaustion of tragedy in the first four acts of *Henry VIII*—a prominent characteristic
of Shakespearean romance—and the emergence in Act V of the
characteristically romance experience beyond tragedy. Like Felperin, Milward wishes to view *Henry VIII* only within the framework of history and realistic dramatic conventions; thus, failing to
acknowledge the use of romance conventions, Milward inevitably
concludes that the fifth act lacks "justification in terms of character" and is, finally, a "superficial" effort by "an inferior dramatist."
Nevertheless, if we backtrack for a few moments, I think we can
see how the first four acts do prepare us for the fifth act.

Linked with the falls of Buckingham, Wolsey, and Katherine
there occurs the steady erosion of papal authority and the rise of
Protestantism which is officially announced in the fifth act by Cranmer at the christening of the baby, Elizabeth. Wolsey is obviously
the focus of Catholicism in the first four acts, and until his fall the
play voices a streak of anti-Catholic commentary. At the same time,
as we shall see, Anne Bullen and Cranmer are continually associated
with Protestantism; just as important, because Henry sides with
Cranmer and Anne, the play's religious movement logically, albeit
anachronistically, foretells and endorses the rise of Protestantism.
That is, the fall of Wolsey and Henry's divorce from Katherine represent the end of papal authority, as well as the end of tragedy, and
the rise of Protestantism supports the play's version of romance.
Thus the "complete *volte-face*" is, in fact, an important part of the
play's intention.

As early as I.i, Wolsey is used as the focus of the play's anti-
Catholicism. Buckingham associates him with the devil (I.i.52),
perhaps anticipating Wolsey's own remark about falling "like Lucifer" (III.ii.371), and Buckingham also calls him "This holy
fox, / Or wolf" (I.i.158-59). Abergavey reinforces the association
of Wolsey with the devil when he says:

> I cannot tell
> What heaven hath given him—let some graver eye

Pierce into that—but I can see his pride
Peep through each part of him. Whence has he that?
If not from hell, the devil is a niggard,
Or has given all before, and he begins
A new hell in himself. (I.i.66-72)

In II.ii Wolsey is again likened to the devil, only this time the frame
of reference extends to the pope and implies Henry's subsequent
break with the pope. The Lord Chamberlain says that "Heaven will
one day open / The King's eyes, that so long have slept upon / This
bold bad man," to which Suffolk provocatively responds, "And
free us from his slavery" (II.ii.41-43)—an echo perhaps of Foxe's
"Babylonish captivity." Norfolk then says "We had need
pray, / And heartily, for our deliverance" from Wolsey (44-45),
and Suffolk sums up the anti-Catholic (or at least anti-Papist) fervor
of this exchange when he declares; "I knew him, and I know him;
so I leave him / To him that made him proud, the Pope" (54-55).
Significantly, at the end of the phrase "the Pope" Samuel Schoenbaum enters a textual note which reads, "(the expected reference
would be to the devil)."[19] What these quotations suggest is an
equivalence between Wolsey, the devil, pride, and the pope, and
such an equivalence continues throughout the first four acts. It is no
wonder that even Henry concludes Act II by saying "I abhor / This
dilatory sloth and tricks of Rome."

Katherine—who rejects Wolsey's but not the pope's authority—
also attacks the lack of "Christian counsel" brought her by Wolsey
and Campeius, saying to them: "Holy men I thought ye, / Upon
my soul, two reverend cardinal virtues; / But cardinal sins and hol-
low hearts I fear ye" (III.i.102-4). Later she tells them, "Ye have
angels' faces, but heaven knows your hearts" (145), which is a version of Henry's later criticism of Wolsey just before he strips him of
power: "'Tis well said again, / And 'tis a kind of good deed to say
well, / And yet words are no deeds" (III.ii.152-54). Indeed,
Henry's rejection of Wolsey's words may allude to the Lord Chamberlain's earlier observation that Wolsey "hath a witchcraft / Over
the king in's tongue" (III.ii.18-19). But the most cruelly anti-Cath-

olic section of the play occurs right after Wolsey has fallen from power. Surrey, who is Buckingham's son-in-law, unremittingly attacks Wolsey, calling him "a proud traitor, priest" (III.ii.252), "Thou scarlet sin" (255), "a piece of scarlet" (280), and he concludes his attack on Wolsey, exclaiming "I'll startle you / Worse than the sacring bell, when the brown wench / Lay kissing in your arms, Lord Cardinal" (294-96)—the last phrase continuing the play's pun on "carnal," the Elizabethan pronunciation of "cardinal," as Samuel Schoenbaum has noted.[20]

Still, if Wolsey is the center, both as the object and primary influence, of the play's version of tragedy, we need also to notice that two of the people whom he attacks—Anne and Cranmer—are just as clearly associated, not just with Henry's Act of Supremacy, but with the emergence of Protestantism. Historically they occupy significant roles which ultimately tie into romance conventions. For example, the first time we hear of Cranmer, who died a Protestant martyr, he is at once defined against Catholicism and invested with a symbolic significance which aligns him with the oracles of comfort that recur in Shakespeare's romances. I earlier quoted Henry's lines about the "dilatory sloth and tricks of Rome," but these lines then continue: "My learned and well-belovéd servant, Cranmer, / Prithee return; with thy approach, I know, / My comfort comes along" (II.iv.239-47). Of course, skeptics might refer to Cranmer's "comfort" as his approval of Henry's divorce, for historically Cranmer was in Europe seeking a favorable opinion from various universities of Henry's divorce (an activity further alluded to in III.ii.63-67). There is no question, as A. F. Pollard has observed, that "of all the incidents affecting Cranmer's life the most important is the divorce of Catherine of Aragon. That divorce and its ramifications were the web into which the threads of Cranmer's life were woven."[21] But the extent of Cranmer's dramatic significance and the source of his "comfort" exceed his involvement with and approval of Henry's divorce; and this may be why the play minimizes his direct contact with the divorce proceedings.

What the play emphasizes in the first four acts is Cranmer's Protestant standing—Shakespeare's audience would know that

Cranmer died a Protestant martyr—and his association with Anne Bullen and the baby Elizabeth. These three characters represent the play's alternative to the tragic fall of papal authority. Historians, for example, have speculated that Cranmer was at one time chaplain to Anne Bullen's family, though the evidence is inconclusive. But Cranmer was, in historical fact, Elizabeth's godfather; as Archbishop of Canterbury he did in fact preside over the implementation of Anglican doctrine; and his second marriage was to a Lutheran woman, who was the niece of the German Lutheran minister, Osiander.[22] Indeed, the play's early references to Lutheranism and heresy are the key to Cranmer's historical and symbolic significance in the play. Even if Henry historically remained a Catholic, the ultimate source of Cranmer's "comfort" is the rise of Protestantism which the birth of Elizabeth symbolically authenticates.

In fact, it is Wolsey who sums up the historical and symbolic significance of Anne Bullen and Cranmer when, in an aside, he says:

> yet I know her for
> A spleeny Lutheran, and not wholesome to
> Our cause, that she should lie i' th' bosom of
> Our hard-rul'd king. Again, there is sprung up
> An heretic, an arch-one, Cranmer one
> Hath crawl'd into the favor of the King,
> And is his oracle. (III.ii.98-104)

We need not take the word "Lutheran" altogether literally, for it is a kind of catch-all term for anti-Papist. A. F. Pollard has observed that "not everyone who was called Lutheran in England adopted the doctrines of Wittenberg; the phrase was a generic term used to express any sort of hostility to Rome or the clergy, and even the possession of the Bible in English [Cranmer was clearly associated with English translations of scripture] was sometimes sufficient to make its owner a Lutheran suspect."[23] Furthermore, C. W. Dugmore has argued that "during the twenties and early thirties of the sixteenth century, the teaching of Martin Luther spread across the channel, and Lutheran books were imported into England. The authorities smelled 'Lutheranism' everywhere." Interestingly, Foxe also talks of the Catholic association of heresy and Lutheranism, and attacks such a linkage by saying: "If it be heresy not to acknowledge the pope as supreme head of the church, then St. Paul was an heretic and a stark Lutheran, which, having the scriptures, yet never attributed that to the pope, nor to Peter himself, to be supreme head of the church" (Foxe, I:xiv).

Yet the historical and symbolic point is that Anne Bullen and Cranmer are explicitly linked with one another and, just as important, with Protestantism. If, as Wolsey says, Cranmer is Henry's "oracle," then that oracle is fulfilled only with the ascendancy of a Protestant ethos in Act V and its promised fulfillment in the Age of Elizabeth. That the play anticipates in its early acts the emergence of a Protestant oracle is evident both in the two allusions to Elizabeth and in the general dramatic attributes attached to Anne Bullen. Seemingly from out of nowhere, the Lord Chamberlain in II.iii says of Anne: "and who knows yet / But from this lady may proceed a gem / To lighten all this isle" (II.iii.77-79). The metaphor of a gem casting light is important when we recall that Wolsey is associated with the devil and darkness. Again in III.ii, Suffolk comments on Anne: "I persuade me, from her / Will fall some blessing to this land, which shall / In it be memoriz'd" (III.ii.50-52). Apparently because of her symbolic role as the progenitress of Elizabeth and, by implication, of Protestantism, Anne is invested in IV.i, the scene of her coronation, with divine attributes. The Second Gentleman, looking on the new queen, exclaims: "Heaven bless thee! / Thou hast the sweetest face I ever look'd on. / Sir, as I have a soul, she is an angel" (IV.i.42-44); and the Third Gentleman says, "At length her Grace rose, and with modest paces / Came to the altar, where she kneel'd, and saint-like / Cast her fair eyes to heaven, and pray'd devoutly" (82-84).

The point, then, is that the first four acts do prepare the way for the fifth act, and they do so by employing a double movement which traces both the fall of papal authority and the rise of a Protestant order symbolically associated with Cranmer, Anne, and Elizabeth. The fifth act absorbs all the prior historic tragedies in a strongly providential manner reminiscent of the basic design of Shakespeare's romances. Several commentators have associated Katherine with Hermione of *The Winter's Tale,* and to some extent their tragic ordeals are quite similar. But the more important parallels, and the ones that display *Henry VIII's* romance absorption of tragedy, have to do with the movement beyond tragedy in the two plays.

For example, the opening of IV.i in *Henry VIII* displays the same romance turn away from tragedy that occurs in III.iii of *The Winter's Tale.* The two gentlemen who witnessed the fall of Buckingham in Act II now announce a shift in dramatic emphasis:

> *2 Gent.*   At our last encounter
> The Duke of Buckingham came from his trial.
> *1 Gent.* 'Tis very true; but that time offer'd sorrow;
> This, general joy. (IV.i.4-7)

These lines sound very much like those of the shepherd in III.iii of *The Winter's Tale*: "Heavy matters, heavy matters! But look thee here, boy. Now bless thyself; thou met'st with things dying, I with things new born" (III.iii.112-14). Moreover, the description by the three gentlemen in IV.i of Anne's coronation, especially its ecstatic emphasis on joy, sounds like the gentlemen's report in V.ii of *The Winter's Tale* when Perdita and Leontes are reunited. Henry himself in V.iv.63-68 is placed as a participant in a romance experience in much the same way that Leontes is transported by the statue scene in V.iii of *The Winter's Tale.* And though I can readily understand why H. M. Richmond has suggested that Katherine is the norm of *Henry VIII,* I believe a stronger case can be made for Cranmer because he, like Paulina at the end of *The Winter's Tale,* emerges as the spokesman—he speaks what Henry calls "This oracle of comfort" (V.iv.66)—of the romance experience beyond tragedy.

Many commentators have noted that the principal literary source of Act V is Foxe's *Acts and Monuments,* and many have observed also that Henry VIII is reduced to a rather passive role in Act V. Correspondingly, Cranmer's trial becomes the dramatic center of interest of this act, and his survival and prophecy summarize the providential import of the play. These characteristics serve to emphasize my basic contention that the play attempts to use historical events to verify the literary experience of romance in much the same way that Foxe uses the reign of Henry VIII as a way of celebrating the Age of Elizabeth. Indeed, like Foxe, Shakespeare ultimately emphasizes Cranmer and his trial because it is he, not Henry, who symbolically completes the break with Rome and forecasts the rise of Protestantism under Elizabeth.

For example, V.i begins with Gardiner attacking Anne, Cranmer, and Cromwell. He wishes Anne "grubb'd up now" (V.i.23), and tells Lovell, whom he calls "a gentleman / Of mine own way" (that is, of a Catholic persuasion) that it "will ne'er be well— / 'Twill not, Sir Thomas Lovell, take't of me— / Till Cranmer, Cromwell, her two hands, and she / Sleep in their graves" (29-32). He further asserts that Cranmer is "a most arch-heretic, a pestilence / That does infect the land" (45-46), a "rank weed . . . / And we must root him out" (52-53). The scene opens this way not only to continue Wolsey's former attacks on Cranmer and Anne, but to isolate Gardiner as the last desperate gasp of a fading papal order. Moreover, the characterization of Gardiner exactly conforms with Foxe's bitter estimate of him. Foxe writes: "But Winchester, although he had open sworn before all the states in the parliament, and in special words, against the pope's domination, yet inwardly in his fox's heart he bore a secret love to the Bishop of Rome" (Foxe, 8:11). Farther on, Foxe refers to Gardiner as "the archenemy to Christ and his gospel," and mentions his "cavilling sophistication" and "unquiet spirit" (Foxe, 8:35). In fact, the characterization of Gardiner in *Henry VIII* simply continues the strongly antipapal line of Foxe's *Acts and Monuments,* where Cranmer, for example, likens the pope to the devil and then proves him to be anti-Christ (e.g., 8:51-52).

At the same time, however, when Henry tells Cranmer that he will be tried he also says, "Stand up, good Canterbury! / Thy truth and thy integrity is rooted / In us, thy friend" (V.i.113-15); and Cranmer replies, "The good I stand on is my truth and honesty / . . . God and your Majesty / Protect mine innocence" (122, 140-41). The clear dramatic purpose is to join Henry and Cranmer, defined against Gardiner, as the spokesmen of "truth," which truth bears directly on what appears to be the native title of *Henry VIII*— "All Is True." Evidently Cranmer's trial is designed to reveal and define the "truth" against Gardiner's malicious intentions, and the meaning of that truth can be precisely established by comparing a section from Foxe with Cranmer's prophecy after the trial. Under the general heading of "Vicit veritas" ("The truth hath the upper hand") Foxe says of the period of papal rule that "to speak most modestly, not the *truth*, but the time had victory" (8:39). This is an especially interesting distinction because it parallels the play's understanding and use of history. That is, the known materials of Henry's reign are used in such a way that the *time* of Henry's history is finally replaced by the *truth* of Cranmer's prophecy; moreover, Foxe believes that truth to be in "Cranmer's book of the Sacrament, against Winchester, wherein the matter itself doth plainly cry, and always will cry, 'The truth has won'" (8:40).

What then, is the "chosen truth" of *Henry VIII,* and how does it tie in to my hypothesis that the play presents a historical confirmation of the literary experience of romance? Let me first quote parts of Cranmer's final speech which emphasize the truth of his prophecy. Cranmer's speech begins:

> Let me speak, sir,
> For heaven now bids me; and the words I utter
> Let none think flattery, for they'll find 'em truth.
> This royal infant—heaven still move about her!—
> Though in her cradle, yet now promises
> Upon this land a thousand thousand blessings,
> Which time shall bring to ripeness. (V.iv.14-20)

Cranmer then continues, "Truth shall nurse her, / Holy and heavenly thoughts still counsel her" (28-29), and he later says, "God shall be truly known, and those about her / From her shall read the perfect [ways] of honor" (36-37). The first thing to notice is that

Cranmer does not choose to speak; rather heaven "bids" him to speak, and thus he speaks as the voice of providence. Furthermore, Henry's responses to Cranmer's speech heighten our sense of a romance hierophany—"Thou speakest wonders" (55), "This oracle of comfort has so pleas'd me / That when I am in heaven I shall desire / To see what this child does, and praise my maker" (V.v.66-68). What the child Elizabeth does is to oversee the time—that is, the new Protestant time of deliverance from the "Babylonish captivity"—when "God shall be truly known"; and what Cranmer's prophecy expresses is the very "apocalyptical expectancy" that William Haller associates with Foxe's *Acts and Monuments*.[24]

A highly unusual, but dramatically appropriate feature of the moment of hierophany is that unlike those in the prior romances this hierophany is overtly supported by a religious doctrine. This is how *Henry VIII,* to use Felperin's words, conflates history and romance. The historical reign of Henry VIII is used to promote a romance experience supported by Protestant doctrine. In this play the characteristic movement of romance beyond tragedy translates, historically, as beyond papal rule. What Cranmer prophesies as "shall" in the future, Shakespeare's immediate audience could easily confirm as "was" and "is" in the immediate past and present. In short, what normally functions as a dramatic convention—a character voicing a prophecy—can be historically verified by the audience. Similarly, the baptism scene which closes the play functions both historically and symbolically, as does Cranmer's role of godfather to Elizabeth. Cranmer is not just the godfather of Elizabeth, but historically the godfather, if you will, of the rise of Protestantism;[25] and the baptism of Elizabeth symbolically marks the baptism of England into a time when "God shall be truly known."

In a sense, what the characters are asked to take on faith in the form of a prophecy, Shakespeare's immediate audience can take as the facts of history. That Cranmer should appeal to faith is in itself highly appropriate because, in the words of Peter Brooks, Cranmer's "whole sacramental superstructure" was historically based on the "doctrine basic to all Reformed theology—the concept of *Justification sola fide.*" What was a romance convention in *The Winter's*

Tale when Paulina says, "It is requir'd / You do awake your faith," (V.iii.94-95), is now supported and verified by a doctrine of reformed theology. Furthermore, another romance convention—the symbolic role of daughters—is again tied to historical fact and religious doctrine; for, as A. F. Pollard has remarked: "It accorded well with the fitness of things that the first Metropolitan of the Reformed Church of England stood as godfather to the infant under whose guidance the cause of the Reformation finally triumphed."[26]

Thus Act V presents a hierophanic spectacle of the triumph of a new Protestant order, in which the experience of romance that Cranmer expresses as a prophetic act of faith may be felt by a sympathetic audience as historical fact. Seen in this light, "all is true" because the play, viewed as the conjunction of romance and history, celebrates what Foxe calls "this noble anthem of victory: 'Vicit veritas'—'The truth hath the upper hand'" (8:39).

NOTES

CHAPTER ONE

1. Stanley Wells, "Shakespeare and Romance," in *Later Shakespeare,* Stratford-upon-Avon-Studies, no. 8, ed. John Russell Brown and Bernard Harris (New York: St. Martin's, 1967), p. 49.

2. Richard B. Sewall, *The Vision of Tragedy* (New Haven, Conn.: Yale Univ. Press, 1965), p. 5; D. D. Raphael, *The Paradox of Tragedy* (Bloomington: Indiana Univ. Press, 1961), p. 25; Susanne K. Langer, *Feeling and Form* (New York: Scribner's, 1953), p. 351.

3. Maud Bodkin, *Archetypal Patterns in Poetry* (New York: Random House, 1961), p. 22.

4. E. M. W. Tillyard, *Shakespeare's Last Plays* (London: Chatto and Windus, 1951), p. 20; G. Wilson Knight, *The Crown of Life* (London: Methuen, 1965), p. 202 (Knight's phrase is quoted approvingly by J. M. Nosworthy in his Arden *Cymbeline* [Cambridge, Mass.: Harvard Univ. Press, 1955], p. xxxv; see also F. D. Hoeniger's Arden edition of *Pericles* [London: Methuen, 1969], pp. lxxxvi., where Hoeniger employs the term "beyond tragedy."); Howard Felperin, *Shakespearean Romance* (Princeton, N.J.: Princeton Univ. Press, 1972), p. 62; Norman Sanders, "An Overview of Critical Approaches to the Romances," in *Shakespeare's Romances Reconsidered,* ed. Carol McGinnis Kay and Henry E. Jacobs (Lincoln: Univ. of Nebraska Press, 1978), p. 9. This important critical collection also contains the most comprehensive bibliography on Shakespeare's romances that I have seen. For further comments on the romances' "higher order of reality," see Douglas Peterson, *Time, Tide, and Tempest* (San Marino, Calif.: Huntington Library, 1973), where it is argued that "the license of romance allows Shakespeare the freedom to go beyond phenomenal representation" (p. 8).

5. Philip Edwards, "Shakespeare's Romances: 1900-1957," *Shakespeare Survey* 11 (1958): 6.

6. John F. Danby, *Poets on Fortune's Hill* (London: Faber & Faber, 1952), p. 80; Arden *Tempest,* ed. Frank Kermode (London: Methuen, 1975), p. liv; J. R. R. Tolkien, "Fantasy," in *Pastoral and Romance: Modern Essays in Criticism,* ed. Eleanor Terry Lincoln (Englewood Cliffs, N.J.: Prentice-Hall, 1969), pp. 205-6.

7. Robert Bechtold Heilman, *Tragedy and Melodrama* (Seattle: Univ. of Washington Press, 1968), p. 30; Northrop Frye, *Fools of Time* (Toronto: Univ. of Toronto Press, 1967).

8. C. L. Barber, *Shakespeare's Festive Comedy* (Cleveland, Ohio: Meridian

Books, 1963), p. 4. Barber regards festive comedy as a "version of pastoral" (p. 12 n. 6).

9. C. L. Barber, "'Thou that beget'st him that did thee beget': Transformation in 'Pericles' and 'The Winter's Tale,'" *Shakespeare Survey* 22 (1969): 59.

10. Samuel Lee Wolff, *The Greek Romances in Elizabethan Prose Fiction* (New York: Burt Franklin, 1961); Moses Hadas, tr., *Three Greek Romances* (Indianapolis, Ind.: Bobbs-Merrill, 1964), pp. vii-xiii; Ben Edwin Perry, *The Ancient Romances* (Berkeley: Univ. of California Press, 1967); and Carol Gesner, *Shakespeare and the Greek Romance* (Lexington: Univ. Press of Kentucky, 1970).

11. All quotations are from *The Riverside Shakespeare*, ed. G. Blakemore Evans (Boston: Houghton Mifflin, 1974).

12. *Riverside Shakespeare*, p. 1733 (l. 967); Erwin Panofsky, *Studies in Iconology* (New York: Harper & Row, 1962), p. 82.

13. In his discussion of *Pericles* and *The Winter's Tale*, C. L. Barber has noted: "In both plays it is the recovery of the daughter that leads on to the recovery of the wife. Those recovered become ikons for a pious love which finds in them the mysterious powers which create and renew life" (*Shakespeare Survey* 22 [1969]:61). On the other hand, Ricardo J. Quinones has argued "that at the heart of the Shakespearean argument is the father-son link of generation" (*The Renaissance Discovery of Time* [Cambridge, Mass.: Harvard Univ. Press, 1972], p. 301).

14. Brian Cosgrove, "*The Winter's Tale* and The Limits of Criticism," *Studies* 66 (1977): 178; Kenneth J. Semon, "*Pericles*: An Order beyond Reason," *Essays in Literature* 1 (1974): 17.

15. Barber, "'Thou that beget'st him,'" p. 61.

16. Christopher Fry, "Comedy," in *Comedy: Meaning and Form*, ed. Robert W. Corrigan (Scranton, Pa.: Chandler Publishing, 1965), p. 16.

17. Cosgrove, "*The Winter's Tale*," p. 184.

CHAPTER TWO

1. The relation between Shakespeare's tragedies and romances has been discussed from varying perspectives in the following works: Knight, *Crown of Life*, chap. 1; Tillyard, *Shakespeare's Last Plays*, chap. 2; Danby, *Poets on Fortune's Hill*, pp. 105-7; Felperin, *Shakespearean Romance*, chap. 4; Hallett Smith, *Shakespeare's Romances* (San Marino, Calif.: Huntington Library, 1972), chap. 4; and Peterson, *Time, Tide, and Tempest*, chap. 1.

2. This phrase comes from *Coriolanus* (III.iii.135). All quotations are from *The Riverside Shakespeare*.

3. See also Sigurd Burckhardt, *Shakespearean Meanings* (Princeton, N.J.: Princeton Univ. Press, 1968), pp. 237-59.

4. In *King Lear in Our Time* (Berkeley: Univ. of California Press, 1965), Maynard Mack has taken careful note of the romance elements in *King Lear*. See, for example, pp. 5, 56, 63, 83.

5. William H. Matchett, "Some Dramatic Techniques in *King Lear*," in *Shakespeare: The Theatrical Dimension*, ed. Philip C. McGuire and David A. Samuelson (New York: AMS Press, 1979), p. 190.

6. There is still some textual confusion over who speaks these lines. Q1 lists Albany as the speaker, and the authority of Q1 has been followed in both the Kittredge and the Harrison editions of Shakespeare's plays. On the other hand, F1 lists Edgar as the speaker, and the authority of F1 has been accepted by the Riverside, Arden, Craig/Bevington, and Neilson/Hill editions of Shakespeare's plays, as well as the Variorum edition of *Lear*. One cannot help feeling that at some level this textual confusion mirrors the terrible uncertainty that Edgar and Albany feel as they try to restore authority. See also Matchett, "Some Dramatic Techniques in *King Lear*," pp. 204-6.

7. On the ambivalence of *Antony and Cleopatra*, see especially Janet Adelman, *The Common Liar* (New Haven, Conn.: Yale Univ. Press, 1973), Julian Markels, *The Pillar of the World* (Columbus: Ohio State Univ. Press, 1968), and Maynard Mack, "*Antony and Cleopatra*: The Stillness and the Dance," in *Shakespeare's Art*, ed. Milton Crane (Chicago: Univ. of Chicago Press, 1973), pp. 79-113.

8. Antony's understanding of time in this passage approaches the view expressed in *Pericles*: "Whereby I see that Time's the king of men, / He's both their parent, and he is their grave, / And gives them what he will, not what they crave" (II.iii.45-47). A similar conception of time appears in IV.i of *The Winter's Tale*. See also Douglas L. Peterson's splendid discussion of Renaissance conceptions of time in *Time, Tide, and Tempest*, pp. 14-51.

CHAPTER THREE

1. On the complicated textual history of *Pericles*, see especially Philip Edwards, "An Approach to the Problem of *Pericles*," *Shakespeare Survey* 5 (1952): 25-46, and F. D. Hoeniger's introduction to the Arden *Pericles* (London: Methuen, 1969). Hoeniger expresses the consensus view: "About one matter there can at any rate be no doubt: Shakespeare wrote most or all of Acts III–V. . . . On the other hand, it is very doubtful whether Shakespeare contributed anything to Acts I and II" (p. liv).

2. Commenting on the first two acts of *Pericles*, John F. Danby has observed, "It is surprising how much of the substance of the late Shakespearean romance these acts contain or adumbrate" (*Poets on Fortune's Hill*, p. 90). Such a statement, I believe Danby would agree, actually holds true for the whole of *Pericles*.

3. Here I am in complete agreement with Hoeniger when he says that Marina "enables [Pericles] to see beyond tragedy," and when he further argues, "Some creative power at work in this world can take [Pericles] beyond tragedy to reaffirmation and Joy" (Arden *Pericles*, pp. lxxxv-lxxvi).

4. Peterson, *Time, Tide, and Tempest*, p. 71.

5. Semon, "*Pericles*," p. 18.

6. Howard Felperin argues that even in Act V "Shakespeare takes pains to make clear that we are in a realm of analogy rather than identity" (*Shakespearean Romance*, p. 169), whereas I am more inclined to agree with G. Wilson Knight that in V.iii "all old questions of fortune and the gods are caught up into this miraculous reversal which, glancing back, makes tragedy in its short illusion a game, melted in the sun of union" (*Crown of Life*, p. 68).

7. Felperin has commented on the "gnomic quality of the verse in the first two acts" (*Shakespearean Romance*, p. 154).

8. Here again my reading of Gower differs from that of Kenneth Semon, who argues that "whereas Pericles learns by the end of the play that the nature of events cannot be understood rationally, Gower persists in his attempts to impose his own moralistic order and meaning on events" (Semon, "*Pericles*," pp. 19-20).

9. Joan Hartwig, *Shakespeare's Tragicomic Vision* (Baton Rouge: Louisiana State Univ. Press, 1972), pp. 59-60.

CHAPTER FOUR

1. Northrop Frye, *A Natural Perspective* (New York: Columbia Univ. Press, 1965), p. 65.

2. Frank Kermode, *William Shakespeare: The Final Plays* (London: Longman's, 1963), pp. 28-29; F. D. Hoeniger, "Irony and Romance in *Cymbeline*," *SEL* 2 (1962): 221-22; Frye, *Natural Perspective*, p. 67.

3. See Evans's illuminating chapter on *Cymbeline* in *Shakespeare's Comedies* (Oxford: Clarendon, 1960). Some other responses to the presence of discrepancy in *Cymbeline* range from E. M. W. Tillyard's idea that Shakespeare's principal desire was "to express his sense of the different worlds we live in" (*Shakespeare's Last Plays*, p. 71) to J. M. Nosworthy's assertion that "the truth is that the Shakespeare of *Cymbeline* was a man in search of a style" (Arden *Cymbeline*, p. lxiii).

4. In his essay "Noble Virtue in 'Cymbeline,'" *Shakespeare Survey* 29 (1976): 51-61, James Siemon quite properly argues that "the judgment of Posthumus's worth in I,i is at odds with much of the play's action" (p. 61).

5. Norman Rabkin, *Shakespeare and the Common Understanding* (New York: Macmillan, 1968), pp. 209-11.

6. Robert G. Hunter, *Shakespeare and the Comedy of Forgiveness* (New York: Columbia Univ. Press, 1966), pp. 143-44.

7. Other Christian readings of *Cymbeline* have been suggested by Howard Felperin, *Shakespearean Romance*, pp. 183-85, and Emrys Jones, "Stuart Cymbeline," *Essays in Criticism* 11 (1961): 89.

8. Peterson, *Time, Tide, and Tempest*, p. 109. I am not persuaded, however, that the play moves "toward the conclusion affirmed in each of the romances . . . a love grounded in faith" (p. 134).

9. See also *Time, Tide, and Tempest*, pp. 146-47.

10. For a different view of death in *Cymbeline*, see Roger Warren, "Theatrical

Virtuosity and Poetic Complexity in 'Cymbeline,'" *Shakespeare Survey* 29 (1976): 42, 44, 46.

11. On the other hand, D. R. C. Marsh has argued that "Cloten's death has prepared the way for a discussion of the other great imponderable that men have to meet, their mortality" (*The Recurring Miracle* [Lincoln: Univ. of Nebraska Press, 1969], p. 77). This seems a very heavy reading of "the fall of an ass."

12. Marsh, *Recurring Miracle*, p. 24.

13. For a divergent reading of this scene, see Joan Hartwig, "Cloten, Autolycus, and Caliban: Bearers of Parodic Burdens," in *Shakespeare's Romances Reconsidered*, ed. Kay and Jacobs, p. 97.

14. Felperin, *Shakespearean Romance*, p. 183.

15. Hartwig, *Shakespeare's Tragicomic Vision*, pp. 102-3.

CHAPTER FIVE

1. John Taylor, "The Patience of *The Winter's Tale*," *Essays in Criticism* 23 (1973): 349.

2. William H. Matchett, "Some Dramatic Techniques in 'The Winter's Tale,'" *Shakespeare Survey* 22 (1969): 94.

3. My statistical observations are based on Marvin Spevack's *The Harvard Concordance to Shakespeare* (Cambridge, Mass.: Harvard Univ. Press, 1973).

4. See, for example, G. Wilson Knight, *Crown of Life*, p. 76, and J. M. Pafford, ed., Arden *Winter's Tale* (London: Methuen, 1972), p. liv.

5. Matchett, "Some Dramatic Techniques," p. 103. See also Knight, *Crown of Life*, p. 127, and Nevill Coghill, "Six Points of Stage-Craft on *The Winter's Tale*," *Shakespeare Survey* 11 (1958): 40.

6. This is not to deny Paulina's thematic importance, which has been persuasively reaffirmed in Carolyn Asp's recent essay, "Shakespeare's Paulina and the *Consolatio* Tradition," *Shakespeare Studies* 11 (1978): 145-58.

7. See Kermode, *Shakespeare: The Final Plays*, pp. 34-35.

8. Pafford, ed., Arden *Winter's Tale*, p. lxxi.

9. Panofsky, *Studies in Iconology*, p. 93.

10. Hallett Smith, "Elizabethan Pastoral," in *Pastoral and Romance*, p. 19.

11. See Ernest Schanzer, "The Structural Pattern of 'The Winter's Tale,'" *Review of English Literature* 5 (1964): 72-82, for an illuminating discussion of the series of parallels and contrasts in *The Winter's Tale*. Other useful discussions are provided by David Young, *The Heart's Forest* (New Haven, Conn.: Yale Univ. Press, 1972), chap. 4, and Peterson, *Time, Tide, and Tempest*, chap. 4, where the play is examined in light of "the antithetically opposed forces of generative and destructive love" (p. 156).

12. In my view, Peterson is much too harsh on Autolycus when he argues that his "presence in Bohemia served to remind the audience that beneath the seeming innocence of pastoral shepherds and shepherdesses there may also be present the

unredeemed depravity of hereditary guilt" (*Time, Tide, and Tempest*, p. 199). I think Knight is much closer to the spirit of Autolycus (as well as Act IV) when he views him as "a figure of absolute comedy. . . . He is spring incarnate" (*Crown of Life*, p. 100). Moreover, as R. A. Foakes observes, "Autolycus helps to focus the differences between the first three acts and the last two" (*Shakespeare: The Dark Comedies to the Last Plays* [London: Routledge and Kegan Paul, 1971], p. 139).

13. Cosgrove, "*The Winter's Tale* and the Limits of Criticism," p. 179.

14. I am referring to V.ii.28, 61, and V.iii.117.

15. For a more "realistic" reading of Act V, see Felperin, *Shakespearean Romance*, pp. 216, 220, 241-42, and also Clifford Leech's essay, "The Structure of the Last Plays," *Shakespeare Survey* 11 (1958): 30, where he severely asserts that "only *The Winter's Tale* faces the realization that repentance is not enough, that 'reunion' is a bogus word, that the only finality (within the world around us) is loss."

CHAPTER SIX

1. Derek Traversi, "'The Tempest,'" *Scrutiny* 16 (1949): 127.

2. My general approach to *The Tempest* differs markedly from Felperin's view that "Shakespeare begins where Prospero ends: with the awareness that there is a fatal gap between the ideal world of romance and the real world of history" (*Shakespearean Romance*, p. 281). On the other hand, I am quite in sympathy with the critical approach employed by George Slover in his stimulating essay, "Magic, Mystery, and Make-believe: An Analogical Reading of *The Tempest*," *Shakespeare Studies* 11 (1978): 175-206; moreover, I agree with Jan Kott that in *The Tempest* "the illusion of reality became the reality of illusion" ("*The Tempest*, or Repetition," *Mosaic* 10 [1977]: 35).

3. Hartwig, *Shakespeare's Tragicomic Vision*, p. 138.

4. See especially James E. Robinson, "Time and *The Tempest*," *JEGP* 63 (1964): 255-67, and Ernest Gohn, "*The Tempest*: Theme and Structure," *English Studies* 45 (1964): 116-25.

5. As Peterson has remarked, "Emblematically, the play we are to witness is about constancy under the duress of tempestuous inner and outer weather" (*Time, Tide, and Tempest*, p. 220).

6. On the other hand, Bertrand Evans argues that "Prospero's own nature contains no rebellious elements" (*Shakespeare's Comedies*, pp. 335-36).

7. This grouping has been noted by Northrop Frye in his introduction to the Pelican *Tempest* (New York: Penguin Books, 1976), pp. 14-15.

8. Harry Levin, *The Myth of the Golden Age* (New York: Oxford Univ. Press, 1972), p. xv.

9. Though Patrick Grant argues that "Miranda . . . is the very idea of charity itself, embodied at the play's centre" ("The Magic of Charity: A Background to

Prospero," *RES*, n.s. 27 [1976]: 2), it is Prospero's action, not Miranda's reactions, which enact charity.

10. Northrop Frye observes, "What the wedding masque presents is the meeting of earth and heaven under the rainbow, the symbol of Noah's new-washed world, after the tempest and flood had receded, and when it was promised that springtime and harvest would not cease" (*Natural Perspective*, pp. 157-58).

11. Marsh, *Recurring Miracle*, p. 166.

12. Frank Kermode, in Arden *Tempest*, p. xxv. In his essay, "*The Tempest* and the Renaissance Idea of Man," *SQ* 15 (1964): 147-59, James E. Phillips argues for "the striking similarity between the functions of Prospero, Ariel, and Caliban in the play and the functions of the three parts of the soul—Rational, Sensitive, and Vegetative—almost universally recognized and described in Renaissance literature on the nature of man" (p. 148).

13. Traversi, "'The Tempest,'" p. 156.

CHAPTER SEVEN

1. *King Henry VIII*, ed. Samuel Schoenbaum (New York: Signet, 1967), p. xxvii. As a precautionary measure, however, I have based my reading of *Henry VIII* primarily on scenes traditionally attributed to Shakespeare.

2. H. M. Richmond, "Shakespeare's *Henry VIII*: Romance Redeemed by History," *Shakespeare Studies* 4 (1968): 336. See also F. D. Hoeniger's introduction to the Pelican *Henry VIII* (Baltimore, Md.: 1966), pp. 22-27.

3. *King Henry VIII*, ed. R. A. Foakes (London: Methuen, 1968), pp. xxxix-lxiv. See also R. A. Roakes, *Shakespeare: The Dark Comedies to the Last Plays* (London: Routledge and Kegan Paul, 1971), pp. 173-83.

4. H. M. Richmond, "Shakespeare's *Henry VIII*," p. 336; Knight, *Crown of Life*, pp. 277, 315; Frances A. Yates, *Shakespeare's Last Plays: A New Approach* (London: Routledge and Kegan Paul, 1975), p. 71. See also J. J. Scarisbrick, *Henry VIII* (Berkeley: Univ. of California Press, 1968), pp. 386-87 on Foxe's "theology of history."

5. Yates, *Shakespeare's Last Plays*, p. 72. The illustration itself appears in Yates's *Astraea* (London: Routledge and Kegan Paul, 1975), plate 5a. The same illustration appears on p. 177 of William Haller's *Foxe's Book of Martyrs and the Elect Nation* (London: Cape, 1963), and Haller provides an illuminating interpretation of the illustration on pp. 172-74.

6. Felperin, *Shakespearean Romance*, pp. 209-10. From a theoretical standpoint, Felperin has softened the rigid polarity of history and romance in his more recent book *Shakespearean Representation* (Princeton: Princeton Univ. Press, 1977).

7. See Henry Ansgar Kelly, *Divine Providence in the England of Shakespeare's Histories* (Cambridge, Mass.: Harvard Univ. Press, 1970).

8. Haller, *Foxe's Book of Martyrs*, p. 131.

9. Richmond Noble, *Shakespeare's Biblical Knowledge* (New York: Octagon, (970), pp. 26, 255; Foakes, ed., *King Henry VIII*, p. 120.

10. Peter Milward, *Shakespeare's Religious Background* (London: Sidgwick and Jackson, 1973), p. 164. Indeed, J. J. Scarisbrick says of Cromwell: "That the 1530's were a decisive decade in English history was due largely to his energy and vision" (*Henry VIII*, p. 303).

11. *The Acts and Monuments of John Foxe*, 8 vols., ed. Josiah Pratt, (London: Religious Tract Society, 1877), 1: xxiv. All further quotations are from this edition and cited within the text.

12. Jasper Ridley, *Thomas Cranmer* (Oxford: Clarendon, 1962), p. 70.

13. A. F. Pollard, *Thomas Cranmer and the English Reformation 1489-1556* (New York: Putnam's, 1926), p. 125. See also Haller, *Foxe's Book of Martyrs*, p. 21, for a concurring view.

14. Muriel St. Clare Byrne, "A Stratford Production: *Henry VIII*," *Shakespeare Survey* 3 (1950): 127; Felperin, *Shakespearean Romance*, p. 197.

15. Felperin observes, "This recurrent pattern of secular fall and spiritual reformation suggests a close relation between the world of *Henry VIII* and that of morality drama" (ibid., p. 203).

16. Foakes, ed., *King Henry VIII*, p. 134.

17. H. M. Richmond, "Shakespeare's *Henry VIII*," p. 344.

18. Milward, *Shakespeare's Religious Background*, pp. 168-69.

19. Schoenbaum, ed., *King Henry VIII*, p. 83.

20. Ibid., p. 106.

21. Pollard, *Thomas Cranmer*, p. 24.

22. Ridley, *Thomas Cranmer*, pp. 5, 35, 45-47; Pollard, *Thomas Cranmer*, pp. 49-50.

23. Ibid., p. 94 (Haller, *Foxe's Book of Martyrs*, also notes that Cranmer was "the man chiefly responsible for the English liturgy which had replaced the Latin Mass" [p. 25]); C. W. Dugmore, *The Mass and the English Reformers* (London: Macmillan, 1958), p. 90.

24. Haller, *Foxe's Book of Martyrs*, p. 124.

25. For example, G. W. Bromiley has written: "The work of Cranmer had met with apparent failure in his lifetime, but the events of the next few years quickly revealed that of all the activities of the age it was this work which had exercised perhaps the most decisive and lasting influence" (*Thomas Cranmer: Archbishop and Martyr* [London: Church Book Room Press, 1956], p. 119).

26. Peter Brooks, *Thomas Cranmer's Doctrine of the Eucharist* (New York: Seabury Press, 1965), p. 94; Pollard, *Thomas Cranmer*, p. 60. Interestingly, Scarisbrick suggests that Henry may not have attended the christening (*Henry VIII*, pp. 323-24).

INDEX